Writing is not that hard

Empowering the Writer Within

Shana V. Hartman, PhD

SYNERGY
PUBLISHING GROUP

BELMONT, NORTH CAROLINA

Writing Is Not That Hard: Empowering the Writer Within
Shana V. Hartman, PhD

Published by Synergy Publishing Group, Belmont, NC
Cover by Melisa Graham
Interior by Melisa Graham

Softcover ISBN 978-1-960892-33-1
E-book ISBN 978-1-960892-24-9

To Savanna, Gwen, and Elijah
May each of you always know the power of your voice.

Contents

Part 1:

Why Writing Seems So Hard: Unpacking Our Writing Histories

CHAPTER 1:

Shifting the Narrative

My people spent most of their lives
speaking poetry without realising it.
Poet Máirtín Ó Direáin

I visited Ireland in the summer of 2023 while working on this book. It was a solo trip, my first, and I saw this quote in the Galway City Museum. The quote was the first line on a wall display articulating the essence of the people of the Aran Islands. The Aran Islands are a series of three islands that jut majestically out of the "Wild Atlantic" Ocean and are home to a unique culture of people off the West Coast of Ireland.

The quote stopped me, and I got teary.

This, I thought, *this is how I feel about everyone.*

We are languaged beings. We are messaged beings. When we embody and honor our inner voices, just being ourselves, and express that … we are living, speaking, and writing "poetry without [realizing] it."

Yet, most of the time when people sit down to write, they do not feel poetic or even human. Writing is one of the most human acts we can do, but for as long as we've been writing *about* writing, the idea of writing or the life of a writer is depicted as this tortured soul, digging into their deep insides to drum up something profound. The process is often depicted as painful and tortuous.

> "Writing is easy. All you have to do is sit down at a typewriter and wait for drops of blood to form on your forehead." —Gene Fowler, author and journalist

I want to shift this narrative. Writing is not that hard. Despite Gene Fowler's words, and many other common quotes and tropes about the difficulties of writing, I am here to tell you writing is not difficult, because you were actually designed to use your words in powerful ways, like writing. I wrote this book to help you understand why and to get you out of your head and into your words.

First, if you don't know me, let me introduce myself! I'm Dr. Shana Hartman, and my background is as an English teacher, specifically a university professor, and underneath that broad title, I have been teaching and supporting folks in their writing and other English-y things for over twenty-three years. I've been writing in some way, shape, or form even longer, starting with journaling in elementary school all the way up to publishing books about writing (like this one). In 2018, I began using my teaching skills to create an online coaching business as a certified BodyMind Method© Coach—a journey that changed my life! This book is a conversation starter around what I call my hybrid intuition when it comes to talking about writing. The hybridity comes from how I like to combine the practical elements and conventions of writing with a more spiritual approach to feeling my way forward with words. I love the process of playing with words, organizing thoughts, revising, editing, and so on just as much as I love to close my eyes and get grounded into my own intuition when writing, channeling the Divine within, all so I can be a vessel for what the words want to share. I now blend my skills and experience as an English professor, a BodyMind Method© Coach, and a certified ICF coach (International Coaching Federation), with my love of writing and my desire to empower others to share their voices through writing. Together, these inform and support my approach to embodied writing (more on what that means later). I help folks just like you get the words down, coach you through your personal writing process, and support you in your specific publication goals. The book you are holding is a product of all the hybridity and passion described.

Before we dive fully into shifting the narrative away from "writing is hard" to embodied writing is key, I need to share a few core tenants, what I call "Embodied Principles," that we'll be working from to ground down into what I hope becomes your journey of recognizing the writer within you.

Embodied Principle I:
There Is No One Right Way to Write

There is no right way to write, so stop trying. When we are taught writing from a sense of "one right way" or that some writing is "good" and some writing is "bad," writing is being used as an act of oppression. There, I said it [insert deep exhale].

I am writing this book because I want to speak directly to your heart. I want to take a risk when it comes to writing and how I approach writing. The risk is not a risk at all, but simply a process of embodying our true voices, listening to our inner knowing, honoring our unique lived experiences, and letting the words we write come from there. Instead of a *risk*, I see this approach to writing as a relief and a release of what we were told and taught writing is supposed to look like and how we are supposed to create and share words.

However, I know that letting go and inviting this innate way of writing to show up is not easy. When I talk to people about getting started with writing—whether it is creating a writing practice for personal growth, writing a book, or writing for their careers or businesses—they often share this conundrum. They feel split. On the one hand, they love and deeply desire to step into the ways of writing as I describe above. On the other hand, they often hear these voices inside their heads saying that they need to know some things before they actually begin writing. Now, this list varies from person to person, but when I'm in these conversations with people, their voices often begin with something like, "But I need to _____ before I actually write." Then, they go on to list a multitude of what I will lovingly call *well-intentioned lies* almost all of us have been told at some point about what is supposedly needed to start any sort of writing. Things like a clear topic, outlines, chapter titles, a concrete order of ideas, and stories that all need to be worked through and figured out *first*, right? In addition, the ideas must be utterly profound and guaranteed to be loved by a reader. Once all of these are figured out, *then* you can write the actual words, the actual book.

The idea of writing "right" or following the "right" process is what I consider "performative writing," meaning there are a lot of "shoulds" that need to be met before and/or as you write. If we feel a pressure to "perform" correctly, it's no wonder that so many of us often freeze and get stuck when we have to write. If in our history we have learned that writing is a performative act, and it must be done the right way, then we go into writing feeling like we are missing something that ultimately causes us to feel not ready or good enough for the performance. So, here you sit, wanting to share your voice, your book, your words, and yet you feel completely unsure of where to begin.

What you'll find in the pages of this book are tips and strategies and ways of writing that will hopefully free you from the notion that there is one right way to write (much less do anything in life). So, if there isn't a single right way to get our words down, how should we think and feel our way forward with writing? I'm so glad you asked!

Embodied Principle II:
Writing Is an Act of Freedom

I began writing in journals in elementary school, a space for just me, my thoughts, my feelings. I recall those moments of writing "just for me" to be very freeing. Yet, even with this early connection to writing, I didn't always find writing to be so freeing in other contexts. Like many of you reading this probably experienced, I had well-intentioned teachers along the way to shift my focus from writing to express and create to writing to be correct, often pointing out what I was missing and lacking.

I want you to know that you are missing nothing. The idea that you don't have what it takes to write something awesome cannot be further from the truth and makes my skin crawl. It's okay though, because in this book, I want to introduce you to another way of approaching writing and sharing your amazing words, a more aligned and empowering way that shifts the focus from a right and wrong view of writing to an *embodied* and free way of writing. Essentially, I want the focus to go from this external, how-to approach to an internal, intuitive, and aligned-with-you approach.

See, we write for many reasons, but often we have learned that those reasons must be derived externally. Early in our literacy development, we might write to understand letter formation, filling in and tracing lines to help us see how to form the letter A, then B, and so on. Then we learn through both reading and writing that these letters come together to make words, a moment that should open up a whole new world for us. In reality, since much of this development is happening in school, we learn to put letters together to make words to meet some kind of agenda and demonstrate some kind of mastery around language. Learning the words then becomes not so much about developing ways to express ourselves, but rather ways to learn standards of language that may or may not "fit" us. It's important to understand that much of our understanding of writing comes from how writing was taught and how we were asked to write in school. If you've ever had to complete a writing assignment or if you've ever gotten a writing assignment back and it was covered in red ink or filled with tons of corrections, then you are very familiar with the powerful influence of teachers and school.

Our often correction-based experiences with writing in school combined with the relationship and power dynamic of student and teacher can be quite toxic. Amongst these pages, I hope to awaken a new narrative specifically around writing and connecting to the power of words. To move from oppression to liberation through the embodied act of writing so that your important and unique voice and perspective can be shared with those who need to hear it!

In this book, you will find what I wish everyone knew and enacted when it came to writing. Writing is an act of freedom, a gateway to empowerment, and even a tool for social justice. As you read on, I hope understanding this principle will spark a conversation within you first, so you may find *your* voice then use that voice to connect and support others with your words.

Embodied Principle III: You Are a Writer

I shared the school context because whether you realize it or not, those experiences are impacting your writing *now*. Think about it. If I asked you, "Are you a writer?" I'm guessing you would hem and haw with something like, "Me? I don't think so. No." And yet, in some way, shape, or form, I'm guessing you write almost every day. You just don't consider it "real" writing. Interesting, right? What I've just described is your writing history, specifically your experiences in school, and how these experiences are impacting your writing today. I'm guessing what may count as writing for you is a book or a news article, not the ways you likely write on a daily basis. For me, as an entrepreneur and someone who coaches others on writing, I see this disconnect all the time. In fact, I was talking with a potential client the other day who swore up and down they were not a writer and could not see themselves ever writing a book. Yet, upon digging a little deeper and asking a few questions, she revealed that she:

- Writes weekly newsletters and emails to her audience
- Creates social media content almost daily with images and written captions

- Designs and writes handouts, PDFs, and resources for her clients in her programs
- Writes reflectively in her journal a few times a week

Can you picture the look of knowing I gave her? I mean, if this isn't writing, what is? So why do we not see this writing for what it is? Why can we not claim who we are as writers? I believe it is because of the oppressive system of school, particularly around the ways writing is taught and the ways we, as a society, view the act of writing. We often put writers and the process of writing up on a pedestal as something that only the elite, the articulate, the highly educated do. What if we started to think of writing as more of an "in the trenches of life" kind of act? What if we brought our views of writing down off the metaphorical pedestal and realized that it is right here? What if we realize that our unique spirits have unique voices and they're just as needed as those "other" writers' voices are?

As we move forward in this book, it's important to understand this principle. Every time someone I have the honor of supporting and working with shares their words, they always (like for real reals *always*) receive some kind of affirmation or gratitude from someone who reads their words. Here is an example of such a moment from one of my amazing clients, Kristin Bowen, who was among the collaborative authors in *Unveiling the Secrets*:

> *I had another mom reach out to me who actually found my book through one of my friends who posted and shared the book on social media. The mom said, "Thank you so much, it's really emotional but I'm getting through it! While it's not triggering for me, a lot of your stories are similar to things my daughter has experienced with sexual assault and anxiety and depression. It's really helping me understand her and be able to empathize more."*
>
> *What a blessing it is to be able to give words and voice for someone else who maybe hasn't expressed them before! And then, it gave me the opportunity to share with that mom the idea that she could just also directly ask her daughter about her*

experiences, now that she's got this knowledge, because we all have
different experiences.

I just felt really really grateful, and it was a good reminder
of how much our words matter, our stories matter, and our
experiences matter!

What Now?

Keep these embodied principles close as we further unpack what
has made writing seem so hard, clunky, and a struggle. Remember:

1. There is no right way to write.
2. Writing is meant to be an act of freedom.
3. You are a writer.

Write these down somewhere you can look at them over and
over. Close your eyes and repeat them to yourself as a way to shift
the narrative you may have had on loop in your mind. Notice
where that little burning feeling of excitement and passion lives
in your body, the part of you that will be the fuel to your writing
flame. Next, we will take a deep dive into why writing has seemed
so hard, that is, up until now.

CHAPTER 2:

There Is No One Right Way to Write

We go to school to take really big risks and make really big mistakes, not to learn to follow a bunch of strict rules.
Jeanie Reynolds, PhD, Director of
English Education at UNC Greensboro

The Lies We've Been Sold

We have been fed a bunch of unhelpful information about writing, how we write, what "good" writing is, and the best ways to write. Well-intentioned teachers, family members, and bosses have created a sea of humans who willingly and almost reflexively chant, "I'm not a good writer" and "Writing is hard." And, frankly, I'm sick of it.

We are literally born ready to learn and express through whatever language practices we are born into, starting with the cries and coos of our little baby selves and then on to English, Spanish, sign language, or whatever language is used in our homes (see Noam Chomsky for a deep dive into just how pre-programmed our brains are for language). Communication is a vital part of our humanness, our survival even, and deeply rooted in how we connect with others.

Ideally, in our early years, we get immersed in the conversations of those around us, and begin talking and expressing ourselves as best we can for our ages and our unique-to-us developmental stages. We are read to, we listen to songs, we learn to read, and we are both directly and indirectly taught the amazing tapestry that is language in order to begin shaping our own ways of using language.

In school, I often felt a mix of prepared and unprepared, sometimes feeling like I fit into the standards of school and not. This was because some of my language development "fit" the expectations of school, and some did not. My parents were intelligent,

Quick sidenote: I acknowledge we all come to understand and use language in a wide variety of ways, and my very quick and light summary of language development in no way covers all the beautifully neurodivergent humans who often do not fit into traditional, and often oppressive, understandings of language development and use. Whatever our path to understanding communication and expressing ourselves, I still believe Embodied Principle III applies here: Your voice matters. And "voice" means far more than what your vocal chords, hands, etc. can produce.

and neither went the traditional four-year college route in life. I grew up in North Carolina, surrounded by beautiful Southern dialects, *and* I went to elementary and middle school in downtown Raleigh, North Carolina, full of many teachers and students who were transplants from other parts of the United States. I was read to at home, I started writing in a journal at a young age, *and* I struggled to read and write in the ways school asked of me at times. In school, I rarely got to engage in writing "for me" because I was often asked to write the *right* way, with the *right* response, the *right* interpretation of things, the *right* order and structure, and the *right* punctuation. I was asked to perform as a writer so much so that by the time I got to my advanced placement (AP) English course my senior year of high school, I hit a pivotal wall in my understanding of writing that still impacts how I approach writing and supporting others' writing today.

AP classes are those "look good on a college transcript" classes that are intended to honor and stretch "gifted" learners. More often than not, these classes create a wider crevice between those who fit the standard norms of school (aka, white, middle class, capable of conforming to Standard English norms, etc.) and those who do not (aka, BIPOC, lower socioeconomic status, non-standard/dominant dialects of English, etc.).

One particular day in my AP English class, we were interpreting a poem and practicing for the AP exam, a timed writing test that allows you to earn college-level English credit if you receive a high enough score on the exam. Blech. In this practice exam, I went all out. I used all the things I learned in class—addressing the prompt, pulling evidence from the poem we had to read, and so on. I thought I was performing at the top of my game, including all the "right" things in my writing. I also crafted it in such a way that wrapped the whole essay in a spiritual interpretation that I thought was amazing. I had an experience with the poem, I felt that experience through my whole body, and I shared the new meaning I made from that reading experience in my essay.

I turned in the essay, all proud. Surely, this was perfection. The height of my adolescent writing! It was returned the next week with blood-red ink all over it, explaining just how un-amazing and imperfect my writing was. My teacher's comments not only noted what she felt would be my low score if this were the real AP exam, but also how wildly "off" I was with the spiritual connection I made in the essay. To ensure I never did such a thing again, she made sure to include clear language about "sticking to the text" and "not including my opinion."

And, at that moment, I decided to be an English teacher.

I knew teaching English, particularly teaching writing, was about more than finding the "one right way" to read and write about a topic or text. As I carried this desire with me to college, majoring in English with a teaching license, I also carried this desire to honor writing as an act of freedom (Embodied Principle II), something I never truly experienced in school. However, once I began teaching, I quickly saw that the pervasiveness of writing "right" was going to seep into my own high school classroom quite easily thanks to too many standards and multiple high-stakes standardized testing. So I began my pursuit to teach English at the college level, thinking there would be fewer standards and more freedom to explore and teach in a more expansive way. I was particularly interested in teaching writing and focused on how to teach it in empowering ways to future English teachers. Through my doctoral studies around the intersection of race, class, and literacy, my suspicions of writing being a highly personalized and connected act were confirmed. I also saw how school quite literally teaches this personalization, this embodied act *out* of us.

The one thing that pervades all of my experiences with writing and studying writing in school is that writing often is presented as a difficult act. The idea that writing is *hard* followed me, the teachers and students I worked with in my research, the students of all ages I taught in my time as an English professor, and now with the professionals I support in writing and self-publishing their books. We *all* collectively just seem to *believe* writing is hard. But why?

If we are languaged beings, born ready to rock-and-roll with using language in all different ways—speaking, writing, reading, etc.—then when does using language for writing become *hard*? My theory is that writing is not hard, but rather it is messy. And in a society that often perpetuates perfectionism, hustle and grind culture, and the notion that if something is worthwhile, it requires *hard* work, we don't have time to honor the *mess* that is writing.

So, with good (and misguided) intentions, societal structures like school have tried to make writing less messy by offering formulas, rules, and other prescriptive processes. For example, the blood-red ink of my AP English teacher was *trying* to help me by showing me the "right," less messy ways of going about writing for the exam. The idea being that if you learn to write *using these tools* and in *these precise ways*, you'll avoid the mess. Makes "sense," right? The rub is that humans are inherently messy creatures. Our thinking is particularly messy and often not linear; we learn best by testing, playing, failing, and trying again, and *that is what makes us so amazing as humans!* When we actually honor, lean into, and embody those messy bits and processes, our best writing comes through. Where the "writing is hard" part comes in is in our attempt to conform to the very non-messy structures and rules we have been taught. *That's* the hard part: not the writing itself, but by writing in a way we think we are supposed to versus how we are naturally designed to communicate.

So how should we be writing, Shana? Great question! Let's dive into letting it be messy or, as I like to call it, writing as an act of freedom.

CHAPTER 3:

Writing Is an Act of Freedom

Standard language ideology is the belief that there is one set of dominant language rules that stem from a single dominant discourse (like standard English) that all writers and speakers of English must conform to in order to communicate effectively.

Vershawn Ashanti Young, "Should Writers Use They Own English?"

I'm curious if you have ever been made aware of your language. Take a moment to think of a time when you were made very aware of your words, whether they were words you spoke or wrote. My dissertation chair, Dr. Lil Brannon, once shared a story of being judged for her language that has always stuck with me. Lil is widely published, has earned more teaching, publishing, research, and community activism awards than I can count, and she happens to be from South Carolina and has a wonderfully authentic Southern accent. One moment when she was very much judged for her language happened when she was presenting at a national conference and sharing her latest research from a recent publication. The room was pretty full, and many attendees came up to her after her presentation to ask questions, share positive comments, and connect with her further. Lil recalled one particular person who came up to her and said, "You know I almost walked out of the room when you first started." Lil, kind of puzzled, asked, "Oh really? Why is that?" The person responded, "Well, as soon as you began talking and I noticed your thick accent, I just figured you weren't going to be that interesting, much less intelligent and worthy of my time." (I know, right?! What the actual f**k?)

Lil, ever the diplomat, replied, "Well, I'm glad you hung in there with me," and then the two carried on a lovely conversation about Lil's powerful work. Lil's experience very much exemplifies Young's idea of standard language ideology and just how much we absorb these notions of an "ideal language" consciously and unconsciously.

When I ask people this question—when have you been made aware of your language—they typically share a negative experience of some sort. Very rarely do people recall a positive language experience. It may be a time when they were made fun of for the way they said a particular word or a time when they got a paper back in school with a ton of red ink on it. As a business owner, I often become very aware of my language when I spot a misspelled word in the latest email my company sent to our list or notice a word is missing in what, I thought, was a perfectly quirky and smart social media post.

The point is that there are few people on this planet who aren't aware of language consciously or subconsciously. Because we are languaged beings, we are born ready

Quick sidenote: many people have been studying and sussing these ideas of oppression around language, writing, education, and more for years. In fact, I incorporated a great deal of this research in my doctoral dissertation, "Conceptualizing and Enacting Writing: How Teachers of Writing Construct Identity and Practice Within a Complex Figured World of School," published in 2007. However, for the sake of this book, it feels more important to focus less on academic research and more on our connection to ourselves as writers. So, the few times I do reference or cite an outside source, I simply use a footnote to give credit where credit is due, so you have the information you need if you want to dive deeper.

and capable of developing communication skills. Over the years, through family members, school, mentors, friends, and so on, those skills get shaped and molded. Right along with that shaping and molding comes our sense of confidence (or quite often, lack thereof) around our language skills. This self-efficacy is really evident when it comes to how we view ourselves as writers. Or how we *don't* view ourselves as writers at all.

I believe writing is an act of freedom. So, when I work with heart-centered, mission-driven folks in getting their messages out in a book, we work from that common belief of the power of writing. I know many of my clients want to feel empowered and highly value freedom. It's often why they want to write a book in the first place and why they set out to make a difference in the world through the ways they work and share their messages from life. When we approach writing from this place of empowerment and freedom, it's amazing to watch how their embodied book writing process helps them honor these values!

However, most of my clients come to me with a long history and heavy baggage around writing experiences that did not feel very free. In fact, as we unpack those histories, I am always saddened about how oppressed folks feel when it comes to their writing and expressing their voices. Here's what I hear most often:

- "I am not a writer."
- "I'd love to write a book, but I am bad at grammar."
- "I don't talk right, and I write how I speak, so that's a problem."

Can you feel the heaviness in these statements? It truly breaks my heart because I know there are deep roots that need to be cleared, and I know that writing is the path to doing just that. But, first, what are the roots of writing as an act of oppression versus freedom? I want to unpack those historical roots a bit in this chapter and connect them to why you may be feeling blocked from writing your book or sharing your message in a way that is authentically you.

Going back to my opening exercise, were you able to think of a time when you were made very aware of your language? I bet you could. Or maybe you have been the person to make someone else very aware of their language. Either way, because of these ideas around "Standard English" that are often taught to us in school, it's easy to see how diverse uses of a language can get silenced and oppressed pretty quickly.

So, when we think about writing as an act of freedom, I want to honor how there are few things more precious and powerful than sharing our voices or experiencing the voices of others. Whether spoken or written or in some other form of expression, our voices matter. Yet, often, the ways we are taught language and writing in school is problematic. On the most basic level, the goal of writing in schools is often flawed because it seems to focus on teaching every person that walks through the doors that there is *one* effective language for communication, *one* way to write in that language, and *one* way to express that language. I saw this firsthand during my twenty-plus years as an English teacher.

When I taught high school and college students, I would always start the semester with a lovely letter-writing activity. I would write a "Dear Students" letter telling the class a bit about myself and what they could expect in our time together. I would read my letter to them on the first day, and then I would ask them to write back to me. As I read and responded to each of them with a quick note, I could tell right away if that students' natural or home language was supported or not in their previous educational experiences or if they had been indoctrinated into Young's idea of the "standard language ideology." I was always disheartened by how many students would share similar kinds of warning messages in their letter. It was usually something like, "You've got your work cut out for you cuz I'm not a good writer" or "I'm bad at grammar" or "I always struggled in English" or "My teachers always had to correct my errors." And they often ended the letter with something like, "I hope I can do better in this class."

Can you feel the weight of their apologetic words? The oppression oozing from the page was evident, and we had not even started the course yet. I shake my head even now just thinking about those moments when students were trying to preemptively tell me they weren't good at writing. Heartbreaking, really.

So my role in these students' writing journeys became pretty clear: support them in embodying their voice, support them in unpacking and shedding their previous histories with writing, and support them in finding freedom through their words. This is the same way that I support aspiring and published authors now. You may be saying, "But Shana, grown-ass adults aren't college students." Very true. Yet I'm guessing you could tell me five to ten "errors" you think you make in your speaking or writing or all the ways you do or do not use Standard English, for example. And if we dug deeper and unpacked how and why you know about these supposed *errors* and *flaws* in your communication, I'm curious what would show up? How do you know it's not *standard*? The reason is because someone who felt compelled to uphold an idea of "standard" pointed it out to you at some point in your life and created some "stories" around your writing and communication. Those stories are most likely not freeing, but rather creating a slight (or extreme) self-consciousness when you think about honoring your voice and sharing your words with the world.

Lifting the Oppressive Veil, Inviting Freedom

When we notice this pattern of "ideal language" found in schools, we can quickly notice voices being silenced. In my experiences over the years of working with writers of all ages and backgrounds, I have noticed a lack of representation and honoring of diverse voices. Think about it: if you did not enter the halls of school possessing the expected standards of language, then you either had to conform, meaning begin at least writing if not speaking like someone you were not, OR you likely struggled. That struggle may have meant you weren't able to access higher level classes, or you received poor grades. But here's the rub: very few people enter school without some kind of different dialect than this ideal standard that is expected in school. That's because language is a rich, diverse quilt of who we are, where we are from, who our ancestors were, and how we identify today. And the idea of "standard" in any language is a social construct. It's a veil. Striving for an ideal version of language is a veil for racist, patriarchal, xenophobic, sexist oppression. It typically only serves a historically prioritized group of people: white middle to upper class folks. I know because I very much fit into that category and have witnessed the power of my language just because I learned to turn down the Southern "y'all" and "bless your hearts" for a more standard, i.e., more conformist, version of my speaking and writing. The kicker is this prioritization is seen in the publishing world for business, self-help, and personal growth books as well.

If you look at the business section of most bookstores—online or on an actual shelf—you likely will see much of the same from one cover to the next: pale, male, stale. Fortune.com reported that in 2020, "Of the year's 200 bestselling business books, only 17 were written by women." The article goes on to share why this is a major problem:

> *Why is the absence of women, especially BIPOC women, a problem? Because it distorts everybody's perception of what the ideal leader and innovator looks like. It adds to the tired narrative that women aren't daring risk-takers. Changing who we choose to publish and read is an urgent step toward correcting this bogus narrative and expanding business opportunities for women everywhere.*

We can't change the publishing sector or what people read if more diverse voices, like yours, are not getting their writing out there in the first place. To change the narrative in the book publishing world, your narrative needs to get out in the world. I can't change the structure of school … trust me, I tried in many ways from my little English corner of the various buildings I taught in. But I can show up and support the heck out of heart-centered, mission-driven professionals and thought leaders, who have amazing insights and stories, in getting their words out in the world. If you're ready to disrupt statistics like these, *and* you are ready to share your powerful messages from your business and life, I want you to know that you are supported. I see you. I see your words. I hear your voice. You are a writer. You have something to say. And only you can say it in your amazing voice, dialect, and language. I believe we all are messaged beings, and I'm here to support writing as an act of freedom over oppression for the liberation of all.

Now What?

As we continue on the journey of this book, I want you to imagine that *one* person. That person you think of in your career or business or daily life that needs to hear your message. I want you to imagine that you only had one chance to connect with them through your writing. And, when this person reads your message, it will activate the change they've been waiting for, the transformation, the healing they long for. Writing from this place is my invitation to you. Let's get started!

CHAPTER 4:

You Are a Writer

I want you to try something for me. Say these words out loud as you read them:

I am a writer.

How did that feel?

I'm guessing for some of you, that may have been the first time you uttered those words. Ever. Congrats! For others, you may have had a hippie-dippy English teacher like me in the past, who made you say something like this before or invited you to write some essay about your writing life at some point, but you didn't really *believe you were a writer* (even though your version of "me" said you were!). Or you may be the person who absolutely did not say these words out loud because, let's be honest, you don't feel one bit like a writer. Period.

Yet here you are. Reading a book exploring how writing doesn't have to be that hard and recognizing the writer within. So why *are* you here? I believe you are here for a very important reason. I believe you realize you've got something to share, and you are being called to do that through writing. Yet you also feel the heavy weight of all the years and experiences of writing (or not writing) in school, jobs, and such that were not fun, did not feel aligned, and did not make you actually feel like a writer. Ah, there's the rub, right? You have been hit with this desire to write pulling you one way, *and* you have a history of non-writer vibes, even negative writing experiences, pulling you the other way. What's a writer/ non-writer to do?

You start right here. You start right where you are. You get to know the writer within because, no matter what your history is, no matter how much or how little experience you think you have, you are a writer, and writing *is* your legacy. Let's explore what I mean by this, shall we?

Getting to Know the Writer Within

I now want you to explore your writing autobiography. Yes, you have one! See, all of us have been writing in some way, shape, or form from a pretty early age. When we explore the history of our writing past, we can better support our writing present. As Maya Angelou famously said, "You can't really know where you are going until you know where **you have been**." This is where the "writing autobiography" exercise comes in, so let's take a moment to explore your writing experiences up until now.

Write now

Find a pen and a writing space, and write about the following. I want you to go back to the earliest memories you have as a child that feel safe to explore. You'll notice that while I call this a "writing autobiography" exercise,[1] I am going to ask you to think about any literacy practice, both reading and writing.

---

1   Adapted from Karen Haag's "Writing Timeline" activity http://www.liketoread.com/

Why? Because these are often interrelated for many of us, so I encourage you not to limit yourself to just writing. While this exercise is meant to help you shine light on your past writing moments, please do not feel any pressure to dive too deeply or to intentionally cause yourself emotional discomfort.

- List as many memories as you can around learning to read and/or write (aim for at least six to ten).
- List any teachers, family members, mentors, etc. that you feel impacted your reading and writing experiences in some way: negative, positive, helpful, influential, etc.
- List any moments from the past where you felt really good about your writing.
- List any moments from the past where you felt not-so-good about your writing.
- List any experience where you felt like you overcame something in your reading or writing journey.
- List anything else that shows up or you feel is important about your past reading and writing moments.

Now that you have taken some time to list these moments in your literacy history, I want you to go back through and note which ones seemed most influential. You can circle, star, or highlight them however you see fit. You may note ones that are your most vivid memories. You might note another because you can still feel the emotion from that moment. For example, as you'll read in my writing autobiography I share later in this chapter, I go into more detail about the memory I mentioned in chapter 1 from my senior English class, when my teacher used a (blood) red pen to mark up an essay that I was particularly proud of writing. You might highlight something because you can now see how it was a pivotal moment for you in your writing history, like when I finished and published my dissertation. If you want to get even more creative with this exercise, you can create a timeline or a visual of some sort that represents the connections you see between all of these historical literacy moments.

Once you've walked yourself through your history, I want you to begin noting your present. Yes, you currently write, whether you acknowledge it or not, and I want you to take some time to acknowledge the writing you do now. When I do this exercise with my embodied writing program clients, it is always such a surprise when they begin listing all the writing they do in a day. See, my clients are heart-centered entrepreneurs, thought leaders, teachers, therapists, and more, and I don't know anyone who does mission-driven work that doesn't write something at some point in the day. Here's what might be on your list to get you started:

- Emails
- Text messages
- Social media posts
- Advertising material
- Program content
- Blogs
- Responses/notes to clients
- Copy for landing pages, sales pages
- Website content

The list goes on and on, so take a moment now to create your own list of your current writing actions. Use any parts of this list I've created here to get you started, but do your best not to leave anything out. Try to release the definition of what "counts" as writing and, instead, list anything and everything that remotely feels like writing to you. It's quite freeing, so I want you to really go for it!

Now What? Connecting the Past with the Present

Okay, so you have done a little digging into your literacy—your reading and writing history—and you've shed light on the writing you are doing now. My hope in walking you through this exercise is, first, you recognize that just by participating in this activity, you have already started writing, and we are still only a few chapters in! How amazing is that? Second, you are hopefully starting to see that you can, in fact, more confidently utter the words I asked you to say out loud at the beginning of this chapter:

I am a writer.

Because you have been writing in some way, shape, or form pretty much your entire life. How does *that* feel? See, the thing is that we don't have to be any sort of way, have any specific training, or know any special tricks to connect to and claim the writer within us. We are all messaged beings. In her powerful book *Bird by Bird*, Anne Lamott references Flannery O'Connor reminding us that "anyone who survived childhood has enough material to write for the rest of his or her life." Let alone what you've learned and experienced as an adult in relationships, careers, businesses, parenting, caregiving, and more! To put it simply, you have something to say, and I am here to support you in sharing that something in a way that is aligned with you!

Take a moment now to allow yourself to start to see the threads, the ties that bind your writing past with your writing present by doing a little (you guessed it) writing. Go back to those highlighted parts of your past and write about those moments. Take yourself through the play-by-play of the experience. Here's my reflection on a few key moments in my writing history and connections I see to the present.

A Snapshot of My Writer's Autobiography

Writing is an ever-evolving thing. I can trace my "tough girl" mentality to my early years when I was a bit of a bully and was constantly told by my "tough" dad to be my own person and learn to do things for myself. I can also trace the writer in me to my early years of school. My history as a writer connects to my history as a student, my history as a reader, my history as a teacher, my life now as a writing coach, and so on. My writing autobiography, thus, must also recognize all of these histories, so I write this as a way to illustrate some of those syncs, some of those connections, that I feel are impacting how I show up as a writer today.

Connection 1: Mrs. Peterson[2] and the Superhero Ice Cream Story

Mrs. Peterson was never my biggest fan, seeing as I was a bit of a bullheaded fourth grader and didn't deal with authority very well—from teachers or my peers. But something happened the day I wrote a short story about a group of ice cream superheroes. I have it saved in a scrapbook tucked away in a plastic bin in a closet. I don't remember all of it, but I know there was a damsel in distress and a villain, and a hero (Rocky Road, if I remember correctly). I even wrote in cursive, which I now hate and cannot remotely remember how to do. In thinking about the connection this has within my overall "writing" history, I remember Mrs. Peterson asked me to read my story in front of the class, and she praised me for this writing. Was this my first publication experience? I wouldn't have named it as such at the time, not for quite some time really. However, as I move to my next connections, I realize that this would not be my last publication experience.

Connection 2: Controllers of All That Is Writing

Mrs. Lyons and Mrs. Doggett are part of why I became an English teacher in the first place. Not because I was inspired by their teaching styles or caring natures, quite the opposite in fact. It was due to their insistence upon "right" ways of interpreting literature and composing a writing assignment. First, there was my seventh grade language arts teacher, Mrs. Lyons. As I walked into her room on any given day, I could feel her mascara-streaked eyes following me. She glided through the desk—well, kind of an attempted glide that had a hitch, like the clip-clop of her heels were uneven. Her ridiculously overwhelming perfume told me she was near. "Shana, what are you doing?" I couldn't bear to look up at her overly blushed

---

2   Pseudonyms used

cheeks and the cotton-candy-like nest of hair on her head.

"I'm writing," I sarcastically replied.

"We aren't doing that right now. Answer the questions in the book and stop talking!"

I quickly learned when writing was and was not "allowed." I think I carried this understanding into my teaching and then my coaching, working diligently not to perpetuate this silly notion that there is a right or wrong time to write.

Mrs. Doggett, my twelfth grade English teacher, wasn't much different. I distinctly recall writing in one of my practice AP exams an elaborate analogy between the tone of a poem and Jesus being nailed to the cross. It was a moment when I was really trying to think outside the box. I was unsure of myself, but I just knew I would be praised for my efforts. No such thing happened. When I got my practice exam back the next week, one would think she used a stuck pig to mark my in-class writing. Ouch. Instead of shrinking away and never trying any such thinking in my writing again, I did the opposite. I swore that I would "never be that teacher" and kept on pushing the envelope. I'm not sure it paid off, but this definitely connects to my future writing self that always wanted to strive for more when it came to writing and the teaching and coaching of writing.

Connection 3: Master of Nothing

When I entered graduate school, I felt like my first semester was spent just trying to stay afloat. I left an English education undergraduate program and entered a predominately English-only program. I had never thought about the two being that different, but I quickly learned that I was wrong. As I sat in my "Narrative Theory" class, which is still one of the hardest classes I ever had, I remember thinking that I was the biggest dummy there was. Everyone sounded, looked, and acted smarter than me. They had read things I hadn't, they had heard of theories and concepts I hadn't, and they seemed really good at pointing this out all of the time. I quickly got frustrated with myself and my work because it seemed like every time I got feedback from the professor, he asked for more. When I gave him more—more deep thoughts, pushing myself to try out ideas I never had before—he would still say, "More, more, further, further." I finally got fed up and went to talk to him. It was a good chat that ended with the mantra that I still chant to this day: "If you're frustrated, you're learning." Not the thing you want to hear when you are struggling to stay afloat and keep the dunce cap off your head as a student. But, at the time, it kept me going and pushed me to write in ways I didn't know I could. I can definitely see a connection between the work I did in this class and my other graduate classes and my dissertation. Now, I find myself telling my clients who are struggling in the middle of their book-writing process: "If you're frustrated, you're learning." They might roll their eyes just like I did, but I know that it is a slogan that can keep them going because they dive back into their thinking and their writing.

Final Connection

I now know how messy, complex, and delightful writing has been and can be for me. I learned and am still learning this as I reflect on what feels like the bigger, more visible moments in my writing history:

- My younger writing self's deep desire for creativity and self-expression.
- My struggle and growth as a doctoral student and while writing my dissertation
- My powerful journeys publishing this book and other books and articles
- My constant desire to help others develop as writers and share their message in their own books

---

Now What?

Our writing selves are ever present and ever evolving. I like it that way. I like to coach my clients that way as well. Understanding your history as a writer helps inform your present writing. This is evidence that:

1. You have been writing in some way, shape. or form most of your life.
2. You have likely had a variety of experiences with writing in the past that is impacting your writing in the present, whether you are aware of that influence or not.
3. Regardless of your experiences in the past, there is an intuitive writer within that you can tap into to support your writing now and in the future.

I'm curious what you are thinking now that we have done some spelunking into your writing past and present. What would you like to take forward? Take a moment before moving on to do some reflective writing and see what shows up!

Part II:

Recognizing the Writer Within

Dear Writer,

We are about to embark on an important part of this book. It's the part that is solely focused on recognizing, connecting with, and fully embodying *you* … your words, your messages, your voice. As I was working on this book, I had a surprise book show up in my neighborhood library—you know, those little miniature "house" shaped boxes with the "take one leave one" signs on them? There it was: Abby Wambach's book, *Wolfpack*. For those who are somehow not familiar (I'll try not to judge!), Abby is an international soccer icon, holding many records during her time on the Women's USA National Team as well as being a huge advocate and representative for women's leadership and equity in the world. In *Wolfpack*, Abby shares a revised version of a commencement speech she delivered at Barnard College in 2018 where she rewrites the "rules of the game" around what it means to lead, be successful, and show up as fully you. Her book inspired this section of my writing because I aim, in many ways, to rewrite the "rules" of writing we unpacked in the first part of this book. As I read Abby's work, I not only was inspired as a former collegiate soccer player, but also found that the succinct structure gave a beautiful rhythm and cadence to the principles she wanted to share and her real-life stories that inspired them.

Yet I tend to resist using the word "rules" when it comes to writing because the word implies:

- There *are* clear rules to writing, writing well, being a good writer, etc.
- Simply creating *new* rules will be "the thing" that helps you.

The truth is that when it comes to writing, you are your own best guide. So what I offer in this section of the book are simple approaches to develop and deepen your own process for recognizing the writer within you. Each chapter will help you tap into the inner guide, inner wisdom, and Divine that lives within you right now. This way of thinking about writing may be very different from your current understanding, how you were taught, and what you think it takes to write. But I'm guessing you got a sense of this unique approach when you decided to pick up this book, and all I ask is that you continue to remain open. These are the exact tools I use to support my clients in going from aspiring writers to published authors! When we learn to connect to the intuitive parts of us, and lay fingers to keys and pen to paper, words will come, and they will be amazing words because they honor the genuine writer within.

CHAPTER 5:

Decide First

One of my friends, mentors, and clients, Laura Wieck, founder and CEO of BodyMind Coaching and BodyMind Living, taught me a lot about deciding, particularly the concept of deciding first! When we are faced with big, often scary, new parts of our journeys, our brains naturally want to know the "how." When we are writing our books, the desire to know the "how" shows up as questions like:

- How will I get started with my book?
- What will it be about?
- How will I actually write it?
- How do I publish it?
- Who will read it?

So many people I speak with who are considering writing their books, and even my clients who are in the process of writing their books right now, go through this and ask these questions! Figuring out the "how" feels really, really good to us. Why? Because our cranial brains are trying to support us. The way the brain does that is by finding evidence that this thing you want, like writing your book, will actually work, can actually happen, and ultimately that it will be a "safe" choice or step for you to take. Before this part of you decides, it communicates that it would be helpful to know steps

1, 2, 3, and so on. The brain craves linearity and desperately wants to go in the "right" order, ultimately to try and guarantee we will be okay. To that, we get to say, "Thank you brain for keeping us safe!"

I want to normalize your desire to know the *how* and the steps to get you from idea to finished writing. Yet, when unchecked, our brains can evoke fear when we embark on writing our books, especially if we are writing authentically, activating our voices, and making these words public for the first time. We begin to think, "But if I don't know the 'how,' don't know all the steps now *before I actually begin writing*, I'm going to fail, right?" Ah, fear is a nasty beast sometimes!

Emotionally and energetically, fear and excitement have the same or a very similar physiological response in our bodies. Now, you may be thinking, why are you talking about all of this body and physiology stuff, Shana? Well, in order to understand the importance of decision-making and the power of deciding, you need to understand what's happening in your body when you are making the next choice, and I am an em*bodied* writing coach after all.

The Physiology of Decision-Making

When it comes to writing, our cranial brains default to our previous experiences of writing. If you haven't already, based on earlier chapters where we talked about our writing histories, you can take a moment to reflect on what your previous experiences of writing have been. I encourage you to even do some writing about that!

Our histories, and more importantly what shows up and what we notice as we reflect on our previous experiences, very much impact our ability to decide whether we should or whether we *believe* we can share our words, write a book, publish, etc. Yet I'm also guessing you have made decisions from a different part of your body. Now, I want to dive into that for a moment ….

Have you ever just had a gut feeling? You know, the one where you aren't sure why you have the feeling or how it's going to work out, but you just knew you needed to take a certain step, make a certain decision, choose a certain path?

As a business owner, this has happened to me a ton. My first business was as a licensed massage therapist. I started the small business in 2017 while I was still working as a tenured, full professor of English at a university near where I lived at the time. I had zero clue as to what would happen with that business, but I just knew I should. I had a gut feeling and heart tug to just go for it.

I built a steady little side hustle with my massage practice just following those feelings. With every social media post I wrote or email I shared about my business and my approach, I grew more and more confident in what the heck I was doing. In many ways, I was writing-to-learn and figuring out this whole business thing along the way.

Fast forward to 2018 when I discovered coaching. Now, this was a game changer. When I learned what it was like to coach and be coached, combined with my love for connection to intuition and the wisdom of the body as well as my passion for writing, it was like the biggest light bulb in the world went off for me! I was forever changed.

Again, I didn't know what stepping into coaching would look like for me, but I knew it definitely was for me. My heart knew. My soul knew. So I *decided* to go for it, and the rest, as the cliche goes, is history. I signed my first coaching client in November of 2018, started my journey as a certified BodyMind Method Coach in 2019, and have now worked with dozens of clients and growing. You know what I was also doing along the way—deciding and writing! Then, in May of 2021, because I decided *first* and received support along the way, I was able to leave my position as an English professor and step fully into my journey as an embodied writing coach. Since then, I've developed Synergy Publishing Group, grown an amazing team, and helped many clients embark on their own decisions to share their journeys from their lives in articles, books, business writing, and more.

I share all of these moments in my journey because the thing they had in common is I decided *first,* and then I trusted that the how and the resources and the steps would emerge. As I decided and took action on those decisions, the steps have shown up time and time again! I want to share some simple tools you can use today to support this idea of deciding first in an embodied way.

3 Simple Ways to Decide First and Share Your Voice

- **Step 1: Acknowledge what is showing up.**
  What is the THING, the decision, the step, the next-level tug showing up? Write it down. Share it with someone you trust. Just naming the thing clearly starts to help you align your gut, heart, and cranial brain. In fact, just say it out loud right now as you are reading this even if you are all by yourself. You may say, "I want to write my book!" or "I want to inspire others with my words!" Whatever the desire is, naming it clearly can support you in bringing it to fruition and making a powerful decision.
- **Step 2: Notice your body.**
  As you name what is showing up, I also want you to take a moment and notice what your body is experiencing. Are any sensations showing up? Do you get a tingle down your arm? Does your heart beat faster? Does a smile show up across your lips? Do you have butterflies in your belly? This is what your body does when you begin connecting to these intuitive desires. Tapping into this connection is huge when deciding! I encourage you to do this often!
- **Step 3: Take a "one degree" action step.**
  Now that you have acknowledged the desire and noticed how that desire is showing up in your body, it's time to feel into an aligned action step. Now this does not need to be this big, huge step that will make all your dreams come true! For example, I am always leery of those who promise things like "write your book in a weekend." While tempting, the flashy methods are often *not* embodied and likely not going to get you what you truly desire. It's a false magic bullet. At the same time, one seemingly small or ridiculous first step can start an avalanche effect when we actually

decide first, decide that no matter what, what we desire, like writing our empowering books, *is* indeed happening. Take a deep breath, tune into that part of your body you did for step 1, and ask, "What would allow me to embody and take action on this intuitive desire?" Listen to what shows up. It may be to go write for five minutes! It may be to book a call with me or someone else who can support your writing journey or next step. It may be to do a kitchen dance party because you are so energized about this decision. It may be to just share with one person what your decision is. It may be to go make an offer to that potential client you've been thinking about. Whatever it is, make a plan to take that one-degree step and do it sooner than later. Then, take another step, another action, and so on!

Deciding that what you desire *is* happening is a huge accomplishment, so whatever landed for you from this chapter or whatever you are pondering, just know and trust that it has shown up for a reason! My good friend and fellow bodymind coach Fidel Forde reminds me constantly that the Divine (or whatever you might believe in) doesn't give you anything that is not ultimately for you, meaning if it has been put on your heart, then it is something you are meant to do, be, say, share. Deciding first begins to create the pathway for all the "how" and steps for doing, being, saying, and sharing to show up!

CHAPTER 6:

Connect to and Write from Your Inner Knowing

I played soccer at East Carolina University, a large state school located in Greenville, North Carolina (Go Pirates!). Before every game, I did what I then called a *mental exercise* where I would close my eyes and picture myself playing the upcoming game. I would envision myself running. I would see myself making a tackle, stealing the ball, and passing it to my teammate. I would also feel my body experiencing this vision. My heart would beat faster, my mouth would open to allow deeper breaths, and I moved my feet a bit just as I envisioned myself doing on the field.

I learned this technique from my dad. He used to tell me, "Your body can't go where your mind hasn't already been." And he taught me to "see myself in the game before I actually started the game."

Since becoming a BodyMind Method© Coach and an embodied writing coach, I tweaked his statement: "Your mind can't go where your body hasn't already been." See, I now know more about embodiment, and I realize that this was actually not a mental exercise at all. This was an embodiment moment.

During my soccer days, that bodymind moment before a game allowed all my parts—heart, soul, and brain—to fully sync up and prepare me to enact the vision I had in the locker room before the game. Then, in the game, I found myself more easily making the tackle, for example, because my body had felt it before, and my brain now believed it was possible. I stole the ball and passed it with more ease to my teammate because I had created the neural pathway and muscle memory to do so.

A similar thing happens when it comes to writing. We are often taught that writing is a mental act. I mean we *are* putting our thoughts on the page, right? It seems logical. But when we think about the words we write, we are actually trying to capture a feeling, not just a thought. The thoughts or words are simply the vessels for the experiences and the feelings we are having that we want to invite the reader to experience along with us. Thus, writing is truly an act of embodying our inner knowing.

Connecting with and following your intuition is essential in any kind of writing. Think about it. Have you ever written an email to a colleague or your potential clients when you were tired, frustrated, or just not feeling it? Have you created a social media post out of desperation or a sense of "have to" in order to attract the next client?

My embodiment exercise in the locker room before a game helped me get into the energy I wanted to bring to the field and helped me achieve my goal of supporting my team in doing our best, hopefully winning the game. Similarly, the energy you show up in when you sit down to write directly impacts that writing and thus the message your audience receives. When you ignore your inner knowing for, say, a fill-in-the-blank template someone said you *should* follow to write your book or share your message, your writing is impacted. Your voice is squelched. If you tune in, you likely can feel it in your body, like when you are wearing your sibling's hand-me-down jacket that doesn't quite fit you: *it's just not right.*

So how do we get connected to our inner knowing in our writing? Well, I believe writing is an embodiment tool, and we need to treat it as such. If you think about it, your hands are kind of positioned between your head and your heart. They are connectors between the logical, linear thinking part of you (the cranial brain) and the passionate, visionary part of you (the heart brain)[3]. When we connect to the hearts *first*, we can receive support from our brains, and then both help us get our words down.

Here are some powerful questions to support you in getting connected to your inner knowing and activate your true writing voice. My clients use these questions when they are looking for a place to start their writing time or even their books. Read the prompts, open up a space to write, and see what wants to show up.

- What is showing up for me today?
- Where am I noticing this in my body?
- If I gave this part a voice, what might it say?
- How do I want to feel?
- How will my writing today help me embody and capture that feeling?

The Power of Embodied Writing

I'm curious how it felt to write in the way the above questions asked of you. Did you have any moments of clarity? Any moments of "what the heck am I doing?" Did you wonder how writing like this and connecting within is supposed to help you write your book or your next big project? Whatever you experience, you are not alone! Almost all the amazing clients my team and I work with find themselves initially questioning the embodied writing approach we offer them to explore as they discover what helps them go from idea to published, and what helps them find their own writing processes.

Here is what Laura Wieck, CEO and founder of The BodyMind Method© and author of *The BodyMind Method: A 4-Part Framework for Embodied Entrepreneurs to Grow their Income*

---

3   I first learned of the "3 brains" in our bodies from my BodyMind Method© Certification program with Laura Wieck; learn more about this topic through Laura's training "The 3-Brain Coaching Model" https://thenewbodymind.com/3brains. I discuss this concept more in chapter 9, "Discover and Trust *Your* Process."

and Impact, had to say about using this embodied approach in her writing:

> *For the longest time, what I thought writing a book was supposed to look like really got in the way of me truly writing my book. And what I think was amazing about Shana and the process is [she] helped me find my way to write the book. With [her] coaching, [she] really helped me embody the message that was asking to come through and give me the support that brought the words out in a way that really felt aligned. There was still effort. There was still stretching myself. And because it was so grounded in the embodiment practice ... it felt like an expression of my truest self.*

So far, we have explored how to connect with and tap into an embodied approach to writing. Doing so is hopefully helping you shift your previous notions of what getting your words down is supposed to look like. And, don't worry, you will feel this vibe throughout the book, and we will continue to explore what embodied writing gets to look like for you. Next, I want to support you in claiming a powerful, new identity on your writing journey!

CHAPTER 7:

Let Your Inner
Writing Light Shine

I want to be perfectly clear: you DO have something to share. Your voice matters.

As I am writing this chapter, I just invited an amazing group of seemingly random folks from across the world to write six hundred words a day for an entire month. This is an amazing feat, and as we are getting started with this challenge, I am blown away by how excited people are to just sit and be with their words. This tells me that we realize we have something to say, something to share, and it is important to get those words out. Because here's the thing, even if the words we are writing never see the light of day, never get published or read by another, they are still worthy of being written, even if they remain on our computer screens or our journal pages. What I have come to learn is that our writing is powerful. And that writing shines a light, creates a beacon, from our hearts to the hearts of others.

Yet many of us hesitate to let our writing light shine. One of the nagging thoughts that often shows up is the question, "Who am I to write this?" I believe there are a few reasons we often hear this questioning voice, and it is connected to the common characteristics of the people I tend to work with. The aspiring writers and published authors I work with have a few things in common:

- They love learning and seek out continual learning opportunities.
- They are very empathic and often intuitive, feeling their way deeply through the world.
- They want to help and support others on a deep level.
- They don't always see their magic, power, and amazingness.
- They keep having this tug to share their words, write a book, etc.

These traits, especially the last one, combined with the baggage many of us bring from our writing histories, often lead us to feel like we have no authority, credibility, or expertise to confidently share our thoughts *in writing.* Thus, the "who am I" question arises pretty quickly. Have you ever asked yourself this while starting or in the middle of a writing project? Right before you hit send on an email? Or just before posting on social media? Me too! It's what I like to call a "gremlin." Gremlins are those little nagging voices that tend to pop up right when you are expanding, taking the leap, finally doing the thing (like writing a book), and that can be scary. Those voices have good intentions. They are trying to keep you safe. They go a little something like this: *You want to do what? Write a book? But you aren't a writer. Yea, sure, you write and enjoy it, but a published author ... nah, I'm not so sure about that. I mean, what will people think? Who are you to present yourself as an expert on anything? Who are you to write this?*

This idea of "who am I" came up again at a recent writing retreat I hosted. As a part of my work with clients, I often host writing retreats because there is something very powerful about stepping away for a few days to hold full attention and space for your writing. These retreats include my other team members, like Cindy, Jeanie, and Melisa, who are also my very good friends in writing and life. We tap into each of our superpowers and bring those to the retreat. Cindy's is yoga and amazing food. One morning during a yoga practice led by Cindy, a special song came on that connects to the ideas in this chapter. The song was a special version of the well-known song "This Little Light of Mine" by LadySmith Black Mambazo out of South Africa.

We were doing a long, slow, deep morning yoga practice with our daybooks[4] beside us when this song came on, and tears started to sprout in the corner of my eyes. Then it was as though Cindy felt us all get a bit emotional collectively with the song and our pose, and she asked, "Isn't writing your book about letting your light shine for the world to see and to share your voice, your message with the world."

I quickly opened my nearby daybook and wrote her wise words down. We all exhaled a little more and embraced the pose a little longer. As we ended our yoga and came together for our morning-time debrief before setting off on our writing agendas for the day, we realized that we really needed Cindy's reminder. When you find yourself in the weeds of writing or not even starting because you think, "Who am I to write this … isn't there someone better … my story isn't _____ or isn't _____ enough," I want you to remember that your job is to let your writing light shine, let your words shine, let your voice and message shine. I share this from one writer's heart and soul to another. Now, let's get writing!

Letting Your Writing Light Shine

Take some time before moving on to let your writing light shine! Here are some prompts I use with our writers to help them get embodied, connect to their words, and shine. Use any or all of these to help you write (and shine) on! You can think of your

---

4   Daybooks are what others often call journals, but they are actually more like a kitchen junk drawer—a place where we stick all kinds of important things that we might need for later, but looks like a big messy pile of this and that to someone else. I reference them throughout the book, but the best way to learn about them is through the first book I published with some of my favorite teacher colleagues, *Thinking Out Loud on Paper: The Student Daybook as a Tool to Foster Learning* (2008).

current writing project with these questions or just write to write (more on that in chapter 12).

- If I could say anything I wanted right now, what would I love to share?
- Knowing these words don't have to be shared with anyone, what wants to be written right now?
- If there is one lesson or concept I could leave behind, what would it be?
- What am I really dying to say/write about?

Part III:

Empowering the Writer Within

Dear Writer,

Look at you! You have walked through part I where I explained some of the reasons why writing may not be (or never has been) one of your favorite things. Yet you know you have something to share, and you are following the tug to write, to share your voice in a book. In part II, we learned how to grow from and with those writing histories as I shared the different body-mindset shifts that can support you as you begin to follow your internal writing compass. In part III, I want to get practical and share some of the powerful tools that have helped me and hundreds of other writers I've worked with over the years to truly activate the writer within.

Remember in the opening to the book I mentioned my hybrid approaches to embodied writing? While hopefully the more *intuitive*, feel-your-way-forward parts of the book have been useful, I want to make sure you also have some powerful and practical tools to walk away with. Part III is a compilation of a variety of techniques I have learned and modified over the years as a writer, professor, and embodied writing coach. My hope is that they meet you right where you are and help you ignite and empower the writer within.

CHAPTER 8:

Get Writing
(Seriously, Right Now)

I see people struggle with many myths when they have the desire to write and share their words, but they are not actually writing anything … yet. To be clear, these myths are very much taught to us in school and society. One of the biggest ones I hear is that we must know *everything* before we can begin writing.

This myth very much stems from perfectionist culture, meaning the false belief that I have to know it all, and be confident that I can implement and do it all, before I can even get started. Just pause and read that statement out loud. How does it feel in your body when you speak those words? They sit like a ton of bricks on my chest, and my brain goes, "No thanks. If that is true, then I just won't bother." Or, like many people I talk with before we begin working together, they have been swirling in trying-to-figure-it-out land for months, even years. They've been working on their outlines, chapter titles, *the* definitive idea for their book, and more, all in an effort to "know everything" before they actually begin writing.

The Truth Will Set You Free

Many people have lots of misconceptions about how to start actually writing their book. They may think:

- I have to know exactly what my book is about.
- I have to have all of the chapters, the title, the order of things completely outlined and figured out before I begin writing.
- I need to go in order from chapter 1 to chapter 2, 3, 4, and so on.
- I need to be an experienced writer.

Just take a minute and pause as you read these myths. When you think about this list, how do you feel? I personally am not very inspired or motivated if all of these things are requirements for me to even begin writing my book. In fact, it's quite the opposite. They bring on the feeling of a pit in my stomach and make book writing seem like a daunting task!

If these are myths for starting your book, then what is an empowering way to begin? Here's where we get to have some fun. Ready? I have one main guiding principle for starting your book: just start. That's it! It's not sexy. It's not rocket science. It's not magical. Just start! I heard one writer on BookTok, a quirky subgenre within the TikTok social media app, say this: "The only difference between authors who have written a book and those of you who haven't is *they wrote the book*."

The truth is there is no one right way to start writing your book. The process is really unique to everyone, despite all the noise you will hear out there that you should have or do X, Y, and Z to start your writing "right." Yet I know you want some support here, so I'll share some guidelines and four powerful questions that will prompt you and your writing, allowing you to expand on and have some direction for the "just starting" main principle I am sharing. I encourage you to stop reading and start writing as you go through these. (Yes, you are starting your book right now!)

Embodied Guidelines and Questions for Getting Started

Start with you! So simple, right? But, often, folks think that book writing is about accessing something they don't already have, ideas that don't yet exist. And guess what? They get paralyzed by the blank page and blinking cursor in front of them.

Write now

1. **What is your simple superpower**? This question taps into the fact that we all have a unique way of being in the world. We all have experiences and choices that have gotten us to where we are today. Your uniqueness can be a great starting point for writing. So start writing; you can ask and write about why people typically come to you for guidance, support, advice, etc. What problems, frustrations, pain points, concerns, etc. do they typically have? Write about those. For example, my clients come to me because they know they want to write their books, they aren't quite sure where to begin, and they want to make sure they truly experience their words as they embark on their book-writing process so that their heart-centered values show up clearly on the page. Helping them accomplish these goals and birth their books into the world is *my* superpower. What is yours? Start writing about that.

2. **What questions do you like to ask**? Almost all of the mission-driven, heart-centered folks I work with have powerful questions they use in their interactions with

others. Whether it be just to help them get to know someone or whether it be their way of beginning to work with and support someone, they have unique questions. This can be a great starting place for writing. So, when you begin working with a new client or talking with someone asking for your guidance, what questions do you typically ask them? Is there a protocol, intake, or typical conversation you have with them to understand the ideas from question 1 more clearly? Write all of those questions down! I did this exercise when I first began working with a new client a few weeks ago, and just this exercise alone helped her begin writing pages and pages of content, which soon became a clear set of chapters. Her typical questions she used with clients were her chapters! It was so powerful and simple.

3. **What are your go-to tools?** I'm guessing part of what makes you who you are and what got you to where you are today are the powerful tools, strategies, concepts, and techniques for personal growth. I'm guessing these tools not only have supported you, but also are the very strategies you use when supporting or helping someone else. For another one of the writers I work with, these solutions and tools became the main sections of her book, and we quickly identified four main concepts, which (you guessed it) became her chapters. Then she began pulling content she had already created from videos, her life coaching program materials, emails, and more. We worked together to talk through any gaps we noticed after putting together that pre-created content, and I supported her in capturing those words. Then, seemingly like magic, a full book emerged in about five months, and we published her book within a year of her "just starting to write!"

4. **What are your stories?** This last kickstarter question is probably going to provide you with the most important and powerful fodder for "just starting" your writing project. What stories and tangible experiences do you have about

any of these core guiding principles, values, tools, and strategies you try to live by, work by, and support others by? What reflections and insights did you gain? When did you struggle with this problem? What did that look like? How did those questions help you or another person? What happened? What was the experience? How did that person implement your tools and strategies in their real life, and what did that look like? Can you paint the picture or share a testimonial? You'll notice that I did this throughout this section as I shared each way to start your book and get started with your writing. I was sharing my own examples and experiences of the writers I work with. Now, you can do that for your work, experiences, and stories.

Whether you are a business coach helping your clients figure out how to create sustainable clients and income streams OR a teacher supporting your students in becoming independent learners OR a stay-at-home mom running a full household, you have a message to share! And your unique way of doing these things, the stories and lessons and reflections that you and those you have supported have experienced, and the heart-centeredness of it all ARE needed in this world! So write on!

CHAPTER 9:

Discover and Trust *Your* Process

What format should my _____ (insert type of writing) be in? How long should my book be? Don't I need an outline first before I can start writing?

These are questions I often get when I begin working with a client on their writing project. Here's the short answer I give: whether they realize it or not, everyone has a writing process. The trick is to discover and trust *your* unique process.

When I respond like this to the above questions, folks usually cock their heads to the side with a look of, "Huh? That was not what I expected you to say." I get it. This ain't my first rodeo. I've seen that look before.

As I mentioned briefly in chapter 5, our brains often work in a linear fashion, especially when set with the task of completing something, like writing a book. We want to know the steps. However, as smart, intuitive beings, we often feel the tug to write our books bubble up from our "guts." We get that feeling of, "Yes! I must write this." Then what happens is our cranial brains work to get on board. This is a normal physiological process.[5] As our cranial brains get onboard with our heart-felt and gut-felt tugs to write, questions arise around "how," the path, for actually doing

---

5   Check out Soosalu, Grant and Oka, Marvin; "Neuroscience and the Three Brains of Leadership." (2014) and "The 3-Brain Coaching Model" by the founder of BodyMind Coaching, Laura Wieck at https://thenewbodymind.com/3brains.

and completing the writing. How do we go about writing a book, for example? What happens first? Then next and next after that? The cranial brain craves the steps. Hence, all of the questions I often get when I begin working with a client on their book. It's very normal to feel this urge to know all the steps, all the "hows" to writing *before* you begin. And to that I say (and encourage you to say), "Thank you brain for wanting to know all of the steps, *and* we are going to trust *my* process."

Because here's the thing: you can't know what you want to write until you begin writing. I'll say that again for the people in the back.

You can't know what you want to write until you begin writing.

What I mean is that the words come as you embody and enact the process and action of writing itself, whether that's moving your pen across the page, clicking the keys on your laptop, or speaking into a recording and transcribing app. The steps, the how-tos emerge as you discover, follow, and trust *your* process.

Why isn't there *one* process or *one* series of steps to rule them all when it comes to writing? Well [insert a pause for dramatic effect here], it's because there really are no *steps*. Not linear ones anyway. Not any definitive ones that will guarantee you write your book in just five easy steps, for example.

And that is where people get stuck. Because in so many aspects of life, we are given steps and learn to crave them. It's how we've been taught that most things work. Think about it as you read the following common phrases we hear in life:

- "If you want something done right, just follow these steps …"
- "Make a plan, review the plan, execute the plan."
- "6 Steps to Successfully _____"

Now, don't get me wrong, I'm not saying having plans or a general order of operations isn't useful. For example, I never recommend editing your book until you have a pretty solid draft going. And you wouldn't send your book off to an editor if you only had one chapter. That seems premature, right? Right. There is a "both/and" approach that I'd like to offer so that we support the brain's desire for "steps" and for the clear "how" pathway while also recognizing that each writer has their own process.

What Is a Writing Process?

Well, if you look in a book or textbook about writing, you'll often see something like this:

1. Brainstorm ideas.
2. Create an outline.
3. Start drafting.
4. Revise for clarity.
5. Edit and fix errors.
6. Publish/submit.

Have you heard of, been taught, or even used something like this? Me too! In turn, have you also ever struggled to follow a process like this? For example, have you ever just been so excited about an idea for a social media post or a chapter in your book or a random thought that you just sat down, the words flowed out pretty easily and quickly, and boom, you just wrote it. So where was the brainstorming? The listing of ideas? Or the outline?

One of my amazing clients, Halinka Privett, author of *Vulnerably Authentic* and owner of The Happy and Healthy Place, is the kind of writer, at times, I described above. As she wrote her book, she would get these intuitive hits on an exciting concept she wanted to include along with a story or example that demonstrated the concept. She would wait for these "hits," get energized and inspired by them, and then write a full draft of a chapter in one day or less. This approach was kind of like brainstorming, but Halinka did it in her head, or she would verbally process it with me on a coaching call, and then be off to the races writing. For Halinka, it felt like the writing would just happen in this kind of magically powerful way. When in reality, that waiting, thinking, talking, and then writing was her unique process.

I have another equally amazing client, Fidel Forde, author of *Difference Maker* (and speaker, coach, yoga instructor, massage therapist, and overall spark ignitor!), who writes in short little bursts of thoughts and ideas. When he first began drafting his book, I supported him in capturing these bursts in a few notebooks he had laying around as well as in one running Google Doc he kept on his iPad. He described his process like this: "It almost feels like I'm 'channeling' some message being delivered to me." There's no traditional sitting down for hours to draft a chapter. He just worked to keep up with the ideas as best he could as they were coming to him. Slowly, we realized his process was capturing these one- to three-hundred-word snippets that he then came back to expand on or combine to create the longer articles and chapters he was writing. His book slowly emerged from there. That was his process.

CEO and founder of BodyMind Coaching™ and author of *The BodyMind Method*©, Laura Wieck, almost exclusively writes her books out loud, and I support her in receiving and capturing those verbally processed thoughts. Once an idea is verbally processed and captured or transcribed, she is able to begin adding, revising, and editing her original ideas. That's her process

Finally, I have another client who has a certain time of day she writes, and she just lets whatever she is thinking, feeling, and wanting to share come through, and she writes in her journal. Then she takes her daybook to her computer and writes from those seemingly random moments, finds patterns and themes, and winds up sorting them in her book. That's another process that works for her.

Personally, I create long drafts when I am writing. I include any and all ideas coming to me at the time, not really concerned with how they go together, and I just keep adding and adding until I feel like I have shared all I have to say, all the examples and stories that connect to the ideas I have about that particular topic. Then I shift into a heavy revision process of sorting, deleting, and talking with my writing coach on what's working and what needs to shift. In fact, I'm executing this very process while writing this book! That's my unique process.

Hopefully these examples are helping you see that there is no *one right way*, no clear steps you must follow to write. It's about finding a process that works for you because your process is what is going to write your book. Now, you may or may not know what your process is, and that's where having a community of support and a coach like me can help you. I can see what your process is as we begin working together and as you begin your book writing journey, and I can support you in honoring and following your process, that internal compass, as well as tweaking and shoring up your process if needed. See, just because there is no one right way or super definitive steps to follow doesn't mean that there aren't new processes, small tweaks, or tips and tricks that can help you improve how you naturally tend to write. So the next time you find yourself thinking, "I don't know where to start … I don't know how to write something like a book … how do I take all of these experiences and powerful concepts and get them in a book … what are the steps …," I want you to take a deep breath, tune in to your heart, and ask, "What seems like my first step? What feels like a light way to begin?" And do that!

A Way into Your Process

During my fifteen or so years as a teacher consultant for the National Writing Project, I was introduced to a powerful activity called "Murray Cards" that I have used in about 547 different ways ever since then. As the title implies, this activity was adapted from the work of Donald Murray, an American journalist as well as teacher and researcher of writing. I share it here as a great, low-key way to explore what you might write about during your writing time, for your current or future book, or anytime you feel like you need a gentle nudge for your writing. As you hopefully have learned by now, there is no "right" way to do this writing activity. Take the prompts and questions wherever you like. Use colorful cards or colored pencils or nothing but your pen and a daybook. You can do this on a computer as well. The intention is to explore yourself and your process as much as your words.

Murray Cards Activity

The goal of this activity is to support the direction of your writing by doing a few short bursts of writing using colored index cards or Post-It notes. You can also simply use colored pencils or label each burst of writing as "Blue Card," "Pink Card," etc. This activity can be rinsed and repeated as many times as needed and at any phase of your writing process.

Write now

- **Finding topics (blue card):** list things/questions that you are wondering or thinking about.
- **Purpose (pink card):** pick one of the ideas/questions from Blue Card, and write about why answering that question or exploring that idea matters.
- **Initial content (green card):** staying with the same idea/question or choosing another one, write down what you already know about the topic or question.
- **Develop content (purple card):** again, thinking of the question/topic from green or pink card, write down where you might go to find the answers.
- **Compose (yellow card):** tell a story about your question (real or fiction), draw a picture, or write a poem; go with it, and see what shows up!

CHAPTER 10:

Writing Is Personal

In school, we are often taught to remove the personal from our writing. When we are asked to do this, writing becomes this external process, which is why you likely found it so hard to write or just "be" sometimes in school. In many ways, you literally weren't allowed to be you. No one can thrive with that kind of expectation. See if any of these rules of writing sound familiar:

- Don't include your opinion.
- Don't use the personal pronoun "I."
- Just stick to the text or research. No personal stories.

Statements like these, as I've said about other writing rules, have good intentions. By providing clear to-dos and what-not-to-dos, school systems feel like they are helping their students. And, in turn, students feel helped because they believe if they simply follow what the teacher says, then they will earn a good grade. At this stage in learning who you are as a writer, the goal is very much focused on a grade. It alllll makes sense, right?

Yet these so-called rules are totally backward from how communicating and, thus, writing actually works. Writing is an act of bringing your internal thoughts to the outside for someone else to read and make meaning from. Nothing can get more personal than that! So what are we to do? If we want to feel ease around writing, I believe we honor the personal. These are *your* words, thoughts, feelings being put out in the world. I invite you to own that.

Now, when we honor the personal, some interesting things happen. First, we usually get excited. When my clients begin their writing journeys and start to finally write the books that have been burning in their souls, they are lit up! The release of good vibes when they take those first steps toward the things they desire, like writing a book, is really powerful. And we can also experience contraction when we say yes to what we desire.

Let me tell you a story … one day, on a coaching call with a wonderful client, the idea of honoring the *personal* in writing was really exemplified for me. Halinka is a fellow BodyMind Method© coach, and she knows how to honor what is showing up for her personally. She was "in the shit" as some say. She felt like she wasn't getting anything done in regard to her writing and in life in general. "I just can't seem to focus," she shared during our session. We dug a little deeper, and I asked, "Okay, what does 'not getting anything done' look like right now?" She quickly named that she had, after all, been *doing* quite a bit: taking care of her fur babies, supporting her own clients, and heck, she was still alive, right? So there's something to be said for all of this! What she really meant was, "I was not writing words consistently to help me complete my book," though she didn't initially name it that way.

I'm here to say that what is going on with you personally is a part of and informs your writing. The trick is to go with it; use what you are experiencing to get the words down. Let writing support you in these moments. So, on the call, I said, "I bet you are about to write some amazing stuff today," and we agreed to do a thirty-minute writing sprint together. Her book, *Vulnerably Authentic*, which was still in draft form at the time, was about being unapologetically true to our vulnerable moments. And she was in a full-on authentic and vulnerable moment during our call. She was slightly disheveled—and as Kyle Cease says, "We love that!" She was feeling down and anxious—and we love that! She was being her fully human self—and we f-ing love that too! After this moment of honoring the personal and letting that inform her writing, she had some amazing golden lines to share. More importantly, she realized that all that she was experiencing was actually an important part of her writing process.

How to Use Writing to Support You

It's easy to think that you can't write anything of quality if you aren't "feeling it." I'm here to tell you that there is a powerful opportunity awaiting you! In these moments, you get to shift from you being the one supporting your book to letting the words support you. And, by proxy, your book gets written as well! You may be thinking, "But, Shana, if I'm a mess and can barely gather my thoughts, won't my writing be a mess as well?" The short answer is yes, *and* that is okay! In fact, some of your best writing will come when you are not trying so hard to write your book, but instead just writing to write (see chapter 12, "Writing to Write") or using writing to honor and name what is showing up. My example of this is in this chapter. Remember Halinka's story? Well, I was writing this part of the book *while* my client was doing her writing sprint about being "in the shit." Her honoring her feelings allowed me to get inspired and honor mine, and this part of the chapter showed up. How meta cool is that? When you continue to put pressure on yourself to make sure every line has the exact words that will go in the final version of your book, you will stay stuck. When you write to write, honor what is showing up as it's showing up, and let the writing come as it wants to in the moment, some amazingly magical content shows up!

Here are ways to honor the personal, letting the writing support you:

- **Writing sprints**. A writing sprint is when you set a timer for a designated time of your choosing and put your fingers to keys or pen to paper, and let the words fly. I recommend at least five minutes, but no more than thirty to forty-five minutes for a sprint. Remember, sprints are meant to be short bursts of writing, not long swaths of time. If your timer goes off, and you feel like you've got more to say and more time to get it down, then you can easily set another timer and complete another sprint. I am writing this in a thirty-minute sprint right now, and I've already written about 837 words! Small chunks of time can generate lots of content!

- **Personifying the words**. Often, we think we need to know the words before they emerge on the page. Instead, try asking the following and letting your words guide your writing:
  - What needs to be written today?
  - What are my words asking of me today?
  - What do the words need to say?
  - What ideas are asking to come forward?

  Yes, it's a variation of a similar idea, but asking it in these slightly different ways might produce some really cool results. Take a moment to close your eyes, take some deep breaths, ask these questions, and see what wants to show up.

- **Shitty first draft.** Anne Lamott, a keep-it-real writer and woman I continually draw inspiration from, writes about the importance of creating a "shitty first draft" in her well-known book on writing, *Bird by Bird: Some Instructions on Writing and Life*. She shares, "For me and most of the other writers I know, writing is not rapturous. In fact, the only way I can get anything written at all is to write really, really shitty first drafts." She goes on to explain that this is the "child's draft where you let it all pour out and then let it romp all over the place, knowing that no one is going to see it and that you can shape it later." Giving yourself permission to write terribly, letting whatever words want to show up just show up, worrying about nothing but getting words down is one of the most powerful tools you can use to honor yourself, the personal, and just write like you!

CHAPTER 11:

The Mess Is the Book

We often have the notion that writing a book is a "neat and tidy" process. You get a burst of ideas. You then write down the burst of ideas in all the glorious details needed (and in the proper, logical order from the start). You polish those words up, and you hit publish. Then a lovely, shiny book with a brilliant cover shows up to your house and hopefully also to those who bought your book.

Where do we learn this? Well, I have a theory that we base such beliefs off the literal books sitting on our bookshelves. What we see as we scan the shelves are rows of neat and tidy final products— *the* books. The ones with the cool covers, the perfect words, the amazing messages. That is often our only understanding of what books are—those final versions we enjoy so much.

Yet I know personally that every time I sit down to write, there is a highly variable mix of events that happen, and none of those events feels neat or tidy, nor shiny or polished. One of my clients shared a great Instagram post one time that visually juxtaposed what she thought writing her book would look like with what it actually looked like. What she thought it would look like:

- Calm time at the computer
- Lit candle
- Cup of tea nearby

- Fingers working gracefully over the keys until she decided to stop for the day or moment
- Plenty of ideas and words flowing with ease onto the page

What she was really experiencing:

- Procrasti-cleaning and vacuuming the house
- Throwing a dance party
- Staring out the window
- Scrolling social media
- Pretty much anything *but* writing

The point is that these scenarios—the dancing, the cleaning, the sometimes words flowing with ease and sometimes not—are *messy*. They are imperfect, confusing, and uncomfortable. In these moments of reality, our logical brains remember the pretty, final versions of books sitting on our shelves and think, "Wait, writing isn't supposed to be messy … we must be doing it wrong."

And then we often find ourselves feeling stuck, or we *think* we are stuck. I want you to realize something powerful: the mess *is* the book. The chaos, the struggles, the "I don't know what to write" moments—all of it. These moments are actually when you are going to write gold! But there's a trick to getting to that pot of writing gold. Ready for it?

> When you are feeling stuck, when you are in the mess, ask, "What am I making this mean?"

We have several clients who love to write in their journals or daybooks. They have perfected the art of letting all the feels pour out onto the page, worrying about nothing except getting what they have been experiencing on the inside to the outside of them. It is a healing process for them. In fact, one client felt like she was stuck in her book writing process because, as she shared, "The only writing I'm doing is this messy journal writing. I don't know how to get to the book writing part." I leaned in, as I love to do as a writing coach, and asked, "What if this 'messy' writing *is* your book?" She paused and immediately protested, "No way! That can't be the forward-facing stuff I share with the world. This is all over the place and won't make any sense to anyone else. It's just me processing my life!" Now it was my turn to pause and wait—all skilled coaches know the power of the pause!

In that pause, she slowly began to realize that her mess was indeed her book, or at least, if she shifted her mentality toward the "mess," she felt a great sense of relief that her "messy" writing was not in vain. So she kept going and would send Cindy and me, my other amazing writing coach, a note to say that more mess was ready for us. We'd read the mess, and it was magical, writing gold! And on and on her process went until her book was complete!

See, these moments of seemingly feeling stuck offer us an opportunity to realize that we have control over what we make those stuck moments mean; we shift our thinking and our approach to our writing. We can decide if being stuck means we are genuinely stuck or that we suck at writing. We also get to decide if these moments mean we are on the cusp of something amazing! We get to decide what we want our mess to mean! This shift, my writing friends, is powerful. This shift is when we honor the mess.

Here are some simple tricks to help you honor the mess and realize you are never truly stuck:

- **Stop trying to write** THE **book!** Instead, visit chapter 12, "Writing to Write," and let the writing show you what it needs from you in the moment.
- **Write about exactly what's showing up**! I used to do this all the time with students, allowing them to write exactly what they were feeling and thinking about in the moment. They could write things like, "I don't know what to write. I am hungry. When is this class over? How will I ever find my purpose in life?" Try writing about whatever is showing up for you, wherever your body and mind want to take you, but just keep moving your fingers across the keys or your

pen across the page. This keeps your writing muscles going enough so that, eventually, you will get yourself back into gear and find your direction again.

- **Take a break!** Seriously. I include a whole module on "the power of the pause" in our book writing programs because breaks and pauses are huge in our writing journeys. Sometimes, when we are unsure of what to do, what we need is to simply pause. Step awayyyyy, get outside, or take a walk. Do anything BUT write.

The shift here is to realize that your writing journey will likely not be linear, not a series of clear steps, and you will often not know exactly what you are writing until you write it. There will be lots of moments that feel messy, even chaotic. Trust yourself and, most importantly, trust your words! Many great books were big fat messes before they made it to your bookshelf!

CHAPTER 12:

Writing to Write

My long-time writer friend and colleague, Cindy, begrudgingly shared with me one day, as we were writing together during a writing retreat, that her son had to write a "definition essay" for his freshman English class. He was back home working on school stuff when Cindy got the message and sighed deeply.

"Ugh," I sighed with her, followed by an eye roll. "Why oh why do we still ask people to write these things," I asked Cindy as she dove deeply into helping her son, and I decided at that moment to use this experience as a way into this chapter.

For those who aren't familiar, quite often in school, particularly English classes, students are asked to write specific types of writing. The intention is that by having these types of writing clearly named (and followed), developing writers will have a certain level of organization and structure already predetermined. All in an effort to hopefully just let them focus on the words and write something "good." The underlying assumption that gets me all kinds of compassionately angry is that students "can't write" unless they are "given" some kind of structure, (linear) steps to follow, and specific instructions on how to essentially insert their ideas into said structure and complete said steps.

So the "definition essay" is one of these types of writing and is described, according to Excelsior University's Online Writing Lab, as a "rhetorical style that uses various techniques to impress upon the reader the meaning of a term, idea, or concept." Does anyone else gag a bit when they read this? Yeah, me too. Here's why: when we write with someone or something else's preconceived notion of the format, structure, and prescribed purpose behind the writing, it really is no longer writing … not the way we are naturally designed to create and write anyway. Are there times when I need to use a certain set of words or a certain style to "impress upon the reader the meaning of a term, idea, or concept?" Absolutely. In fact, I'm doing it right now as I write this part of the book. But, when that reason or purpose for doing so is set *before* we begin writing, we no longer are activating the writer within and instead are asking our students, and ultimately our adult selves, to conform our thoughts *to* a type of writing. This often causes a bit of friction in our ability to get words down, and it can feel just plain backward.

So why would we do this? Well, the truth is we often don't trust humans to come to their own ways of being and knowing *and* writing in the world, especially in the system of school. So we create all of these types and categories of writing to follow for these humans that walk into our classrooms because if we don't, well, who knows what they will do, right? Can you feel the sheer terror in letting them, for instance, write to write? No? Me neither, which is why I encourage writers to *just write* and see what shows up.

When you are writing, I highly encourage you to do the work of setting down any preconceived notions of what your writing has to look like, what format, order, structure, etc. it needs to fit into, and simply write to write. It will single-handedly be the most freeing gift to your new writerly self!

Are you protesting? You may be thinking, "But, Shana, there are certain rules and expectations for different writing moments, right?" Yes, of course, but this is a matter of order of operations; what we put first matters. And, if you are not putting first *your* words, *your* process for getting those words down, and following *your* journey for organizing and structuring the words, then you may find yourself very frustrated and disconnected from your intention behind writing in the first place. Let's use an email as a simple example.

When I sit down to write an email, do I go and look up what "email writing" is? No. In all likelihood, if I am writing an email after the late 1990s, I have encountered an email before. Therefore, I can draw upon what I have experienced in those messages to write my email. If I somehow have never written nor seen an email, I can likely conclude that this writing feels somewhat letter-like. I can likely figure out that I need to start with the person's name to whom I am writing. Then I need to include the content I want to share with this person. Then I might end with letting the person know who this message is from.

Now, when I go to look up what "email writing" is, the first hit I get on my search is for a site focused on good grammar and a special blog post that shares the "anatomy of a good email." Yes, an email is being compared to a subject in science. Can you feel the disconnect?

Cindy's son knows how to play the game of school well enough to know that his teacher will tell him exactly what goes where in the definition essay, and he knows that his actual ideas and creativity are not wanted in such an assignment. If these are the kinds of experiences you have had in school, then there is a history of expecting yourself to figure out or follow someone else's structure, the order of ideas in full detail *before* you begin writing. When we come to our writing from such restrictive experiences, it's easy to see why writing something we so desire to write, like our amazing books, gets us all flummoxed! We literally feel a tug-of-war going on within our brains.

On the other hand, when we write to write and see what shows up, we invite our whole selves to become a part of the process. We start from within rather than from the outside. We trust that as we type each letter, as each word is formed, and as those words form together into something someone else can potentially read and understand, the meaning we are trying to convey will emerge. Take a moment as you are reading to notice how that approach to writing feels versus following a specific formula.

This is not to say that there isn't a time or place for adhering to the conventions of a particular genre or type of writing. Going back to my email example, if I chose to not include a subject, didn't use my recipient's name in any way, had a sparse or incoherent message, ended with something like "peace out," *and* I was writing this email to my boss, there would be an issue. I am not adhering to the expectations of the genre of email writing given my audience and context for writing. But, when we approach *all* writing from this way, and we never find a way to release this school-based approach to writing, then, well, we're going to feel like Sisyphus rolling an unbelievably difficult boulder up a hill we don't actually need to climb. There will be a consistent pattern of feeling stuck, and we may consistently doubt whether what we are doing is right or good or worth anyone's time.

"Okay, Shana, I get it. So how does this writing to write business work?" you may ask. One of my favorite writing gurus, Donald Murray, in his book *Write to Learn*, coined the amazing concept of using writing as a vehicle for learning about ourselves or anything we might be reading or studying. Murray wrote this book in 1984 during an important shift in writing instruction in colleges. Up until the publication of books like this one, writing was seen as product-focused, meaning what a person wrote, the final writing itself, and its accuracy and correctness were deemed most important in schools. In his books, Murray, and many other writing teachers and researchers that followed, pushed back on product-focused writing and offered aspiring writers a new way to view and discover their journey with a piece of writing.

"The longer I write, the more important I believe it is to write the first draft as fast as possible. In drafting, I push myself so I am at the edge of discomfort. … Later, it will be time for consideration and reconsideration, slow, careful revision and editing. But on the first draft I have to achieve velocity, just as you do if you want the bike to balance." —Donald Murray, *Shoptalk: Learning to Write with Writers*

"Instead of teaching finished writing, we should teach unfinished writing, and glory in its unfinishedness. We work with language in action. We share with our students the continual excitement of choosing one word instead of another, of searching for the one true word. This is not a question of correct or incorrect, of etiquette or custom. This is a matter of far higher importance." —Donald Murray, *The Essential Don Murray: Lessons from America's Greatest Writing Teacher*

"Writing is primarily not a matter of talent, of dedication, of vision, of vocabulary, of style, but simply a matter of sitting. The writer is a person who writes." —Donald Murray, *The Essential Don Murray: Lessons from America's Greatest Writing Teacher*

Try on "Writing to Write"

Use one or all of the quotes I shared from Donald Murray as inspiration and try some writing just to write. Here are some tips, and I encourage you to make this moment your own.

Write now

- **Set a timer**. We often feel pressure when we sit down to write. Pressure to get a lot of words down, pressure to make sure those words are the "right" words, and pressure to write well out of the gate. To help let go of this pressure, simply set a timer for ten to thirty minutes, and do your best to write without stopping for that whole time. See what shows up!

- **Be open**. As you write, be open to what wants to show up. What if there was no final destination, no place you were trying to get to with your words? What would you write? What is asking to be written in this moment? Let yourself be surprised at what wants to show up.
- **Reflect and observe yourself**. Writing in this way may feel new. After your timer goes off, take another minute or two and notice what, if any, feelings show up as you write this way. How did it feel to just write to write? As you do this more, continue to take time to reflect afterward and see if you notice any changes.

CHAPTER 13:

Creating Writerly Habits

To cultivate the writer within, you need to do one simple thing: write. If you are not used to writing or are learning who you are and what your process is as a writer, then this chapter will support you in creating something every writer needs: writerly habits.

Writerly habits are the things we do on a relatively consistent basis that support us in getting words on the page, screen, social media post, email, and so on. They're the foundation of our writing process. The key, as I've discussed thoroughly in this book, is to start somewhere. Here I offer three of my favorite, simple tools that have helped me create my own writerly habits over the years. Remember, there is no one right way to write, so there is no one right or perfect writerly habit. Each writer has to explore and find what is most aligned for them. I encourage you to try them and see what shows up for you.

Daybooks

I learned about daybooks in the summer of 2004 during my first doctoral class at UNC Charlotte in Charlotte, North Carolina. The class was called "Summer Institute" and was run by National Writing Project teachers who were well versed in "teachers teaching teachers" about the power of writing. The focus of the course was, you guessed it, *writing*, and daybooks were the key tool we were told to use to capture all the writing and thinking we were doing that summer. It was an all-in-one, kitchen junk drawer space for us to keep all of our writing for the course in one spot.

At the time, I was on a mission to get my PhD done as quickly as possible. I wasn't messing around! So, when I learned about these black and white, cow-colored composition notebooks, I was like, "Ugh, pen and paper? Glue sticks? Nope, I don't have time for this."

I resisted. Big time. I wanted to be efficient and capture everything on the computer. Writing in the daybook felt like a waste of time. If I was going to ultimately need my writing to be on a computer, then why not skip (what I saw as) the messy, inefficient paper step? I see this same sentiment when people begin developing their writing practice and begin writing their books. Like me, they are often focused on the task of getting writing *done* and the final product.

While, yes, we ultimately want to get to the publish finish line, there is something unique and powerful about the daybook as a tool to integrate in that journey. The daybook forces us to slow down, to trust that if we write something and write often, whether that writing has a clear focus or not, the final product will emerge. Once I allowed myself to slow down, focus on capturing my thoughts and experiences as they came to me, without worry of whether the writing was going anywhere or whether anyone was going to read it, I fell in love with the daybook, and my final writing projects were completed with ease.

I fell in love with daybooks so much that I wound up coauthoring a book all about them called *Thinking Out Loud on Paper: The Student Daybook as a Tool to Foster Learning*, published in 2008. It was my first published book! Talk about the irony of not focusing on the final product so that an amazing final product could emerge! In the book, we describe daybooks much like a kitchen junk drawer, as I shared briefly in chapter 8. To expand here, the kitchen junk drawer is often that place in your living space that has a collection of all sorts of things, some you know of (like your favorite restaurant takeout menu) and some you forget about until you desperately need it (like that safety pin you need to hold your dress together on the way out the door). That's my kitchen junk drawer. It's filled with a clashing of all sorts of things I put in there when it has no other place to go, yet I know I may need one day: pens, pencils, stapler, tape, sticky notes, business cards, flashlight, mini screwdriver, paperclips, twist ties. It's the MacGyver of drawers in my home (if you don't get this reference, then do a quick Google search to catch up)! The daybook is like my kitchen junk drawer because it's a place to:

1. Capture things in the moment, like a quirky sentence for this book that I thought of while waiting in line at the coffee shop.
2. Hold things for later, like the title for this book that I didn't know I wrote a few months ago in my daybook.
3. Breathe my words into a place for now so I can breathe them out in an email or social media post or my book later (or not … sometimes my daybook writing is just for me).

There is no right way to keep or maintain a daybook. The idea for using a daybook is simple:

1. Get a notebook you like. I still prefer the Mead composition notebooks. I highly recommend bound pages versus a binder or notebook that encourages tearing pages out. Why? There is power in keeping your words, no matter how terrible or silly or unusable they are.
2. Write. Simple, yet by now in the book you have hopefully realized that writing something and writing often is the number one tool for creating writerly habits. I find my best time for daybook writing is in the morning, but you can use it anytime.
3. Keep it with you always and put everything in it. From to-do lists to quotes to words I love to a paragraph for my next book to stickers from the dentist. I try to keep my daybook nearby for easy capturing.

What happens when you keep a daybook is you see how you are always in flow, always creative in some way, and always writing. The more writing in the daybook becomes a regular part of your day, like your daily walk or morning cup of coffee, the more you will feel yourself owning the writer within.

Writing Around the Edges

I want to be honest with you: You are not likely to turn writing into a career. You are not likely to start and end your day sitting in front of a blank page, pouring magical words out. While I love all that I have shared in this book, and truly believe in the power of your voice, most of us don't have the desire to be an author full-time, nor are we likely to make enough financially from our books to fully sustain our lifestyles (though I can't wait for someone to read this and prove me wrong!). Knowing this, and knowing we have full-time lives that require our full-time attention, I want to encourage you to employ the concept of "writing around the edges."

Writing around the edges is a term coined by Dr. Lil Brannon, whom I mentioned earlier. For me, the idea really landed when I began working closely with Cindy, an author, teacher, yogi, lead writing coach for Synergy Publishing Group, and dear friend. She explains it like this:

> *You know when you are doing laundry, just folding and sorting, and all of a sudden you get an idea about that chapter you've been working on? Well, instead of hoping you remember when you get back to your computer, you write it down on a sticky note or send yourself a voice memo. You write around the edges of your life.*

What I love about writing around the edges is that it allows me to honor the writer within while also living life. Don't get me wrong, I love hosting writing retreats where the participants and I get large swaths of time to write and write. That's magical. *And* most of us are spending time with our families, running businesses, working with our clients, doing our jobs, going to the grocery store, and so on. We don't have large swaths of time to separate ourselves from our daily lives to "go write our book." This often is what discourages people with unique, important, and powerful messages to share from writing their books. You may even be reading this and thinking, "I am too busy. I don't think I have the time to write my book." This is where writing around the edges comes to support you in creating writerly habits, not a full-time writer life, though I would argue that any writing and writing around the edges makes for a fine writing life!

Now you can play with what writing gets to look like in your daily life. You get to write your book, your emails, your program notes anytime if you allow yourself the freedom to write around the edges. This freedom to write and capture words anytime can show up in the following ways:

- In the carpool line
- At the grocery store
- Talking with a friend
- Reading a book
- Working with clients

Now, when inspiration hits, you don't need to stop everything and go write for an hour. You also don't need to fret that you will lose the inspiring idea that came to you. Instead, you simply get to jot down whatever showed up in note form, sentence form, or just a word. The point is to do something and do it often. You will be amazed at how simply capturing the writing that shows up around the edges of your life can support your book and other writing.

Writing Community

As an English major in college, my vision of a writer *writing* was usually something like this: waking up around sunrise, pouring a cup of black coffee, sitting down at a typewriter, and toiling over each word; taking periodic breaks throughout the day, pacing back and forth when the words don't come, and then inspiration hitting again and again, the writer typing furiously to keep up.

Well, friends, I proudly claim myself as a writer, and I know and have worked with many published writers, and let me tell you … that ain't what it's like!

I opened the book sharing how this visual and the idea that writing is hard permeates our culture. We often put writers on pedestals due to the pervasive thought that the act of putting words on a page is such a difficult feat to accomplish. Yet I have spent a whole book illustrating (hopefully!) how writing is one of the most embodied and natural acts of expression we can do. One of the things that can help make it so embodied and connected is being a part of a writing community. Hands down, having a writing community is going to be one of the most powerful ways to develop a habit of writing.

What is a writing community? A writing community can be lots of different things, and just like our writing processes, it can be whatever you need it to be in order to support you in getting your words down. The "Embodied Writing Community" that my team and I have intentionally built aims to provide three main things: butt-in-seat time, loving accountability, and affirmation.

One cannot successfully write without actually writing! An easy way to support that is to actually schedule or join a writing time with others. We provide our clients with what we call "writing days" every second and fourth Wednesday of the month, and that time becomes sacred to us and our community. The set up is quite simple: We join Zoom, do a quick embodiment practice together (think eyes closed, connecting within, preparing ourselves for the messages that want to come forth), share our intentions, and then we set a timer and write! Device cameras often go off, we mute ourselves, and we write together, each working on what is needed for that day. This is our butt-in-seat time!

What we decide to work on that day varies, but sharing our intentions provides us with the loving accountability we need to keep our writing projects going. Sometimes it is the final revisions of our final book chapters. Sometimes it is our next email or series of social media posts to our audiences. Sometimes it is messy, seemingly aimless writing just to write and see what wants to show up. After the timer goes off, we check in, and most of the time, folks shoo us away and ask for the next timer to be set because they are in a writing flow and want to keep the groove going. At the end of our two-ish hours together, everyone is invited to share an excerpt from what they wrote that day. This is always optional and always one of the most powerful parts of the writing day. I can't tell you how amazing it is to receive affirmation at the end of our writing time. While we are indeed writing together, we often feel like we don't know what we are doing, whether it makes sense, and if anyone will remotely resonate with our words. Can you relate to that uncertainty around your writing? This is where a writing community works its magic! The "oohs" and "ahhs," the "I just got chills" typed in the chat, the writing buddies who unmute themselves because they are dying to tell you exactly how powerful your words are, all of these combine to provide the affirmation we all need to keep going, keep writing, and make sure we share our words with the world.

Starting Your Writerly Habits

The threads that bind all of these support tools for creating strong writerly habits is that none are done in a vacuum, and none are terribly complicated. Whatever you find works to connect with ease to your words and help you get them from inside of you and out onto a page is what matters. Remember, writing is not that hard, so let's trust ourselves and our processes and just write!

CHAPTER 14:

Don't Write for Others (All the Time)

Have you ever stared at a blank screen when trying to write? That cursor just blinking and blinking at you over and over? Take a moment and put yourself there again … what were you thinking? Feeling? What was showing up?

If any of your answers involved thinking about what to say and how to say it best, then you are not alone! Consciously or not, you were also thinking about the reader, the audience. To help you practically recognize the writer within, I want to make an argument for *not writing for others* … at least not all the time. Yep, that's right, I don't want you to think about the reader when writing. Let me explain.

Peter Elbow, long-standing writer, teacher, and researcher of writing, wrote an article, "Closing My Eyes as I Speak: An Argument for Ignoring Audience," published in 1987 in *College English* journal. In the article, Elbow talks about the power of "ignoring your audience," especially when in the heart of drafting your writing. Elbow is a well-known teacher, researcher, and writer about writing. He helped create a shift of change in the 1980s around writing to write, writing without the heavy influence of teachers, and writing for the purpose of expression. Here is how Elbow explains this approach to writing:

When I am talking to a person or a group and struggling to find words or thoughts, I often find myself involuntarily closing my eyes as I speak. I realize now that this behavior is an instinctive attempt to blot out awareness of audience when I need all my concentration for just trying to figure out or express what I want to say. Because the audience is so imperiously present in a speaking situation, my instinct reacts with this active attempt to avoid audience awareness. This behavior–in a sense impolite or antisocial–is not so uncommon. Even when we write, alone in a room to an absent audience, there are occasions when we are struggling to figure something out and need to push aside awareness of those absent readers.

So, instead of focusing on the reader in our writing, what if we focused on letting the words out, giving them a voice, being a vessel for what the words and text need? Elbow goes on to quote Donald Murray:

My sense of audience is so strong that I have to suppress my conscious awareness of audience to hear what the text demands.

Think about it: have you ever done some casual journal writing or freewriting that turned out to be really strong and powerful? What if you approached the bulk of writing your book as though it were a casual moment in your daybook, just writing to write? I'm curious how it feels in your body as you read these words. I'm guessing there may be a mix of "can I really do that?" and "oh, that sounds/feels nice" showing up right now.

See, when we write for an audience, for our readers, we change our approach to writing. I'm not suggesting this is a bad thing, as we certainly want our readers to enjoy our writing, and it's amazing when something I wrote resonates with a reader. Yet I have seen some of my clients get really stuck with the conundrum of who their audience is and whether they are writing "right" for that audience. Instead of spinning in this land of the unknown, try trusting the words and letting what those words need to be, be the focus for a while.

I can already see your shoulders dropping and a smile creeping across your face. Now, go write in that vibe and see how it feels!

Writing Just for You

Whether you are just getting started or are well into your writing project, I want you to take twenty to thirty minutes and write about the idea, story, experience, concept, or lesson that is burning inside, dying to get out. Ignore any voices telling you what you should say, how you should say it, etc. and just let it rip.

I encourage you not to worry about spelling, punctuation, or grammar. I encourage you to curse, write in all caps, make jokes, and above all else, tell the truth, your truth. Feel the words, and let them know they can say, do, be, and show up just as they want to right now. Ready? Write!

EPILOGUE:

Now What? It's Your Turn

Girl; write clearly; make sure you have a clear beginning and end; ideally three main points that you tell the audience at the beginning, then tell them about again in each paragraph; write a clear topic sentence; write a catchy opening line; use no more than three to five words in the first line of your caption; do your market research so you know your book will be a bestseller; your subject line must draw the reader in or they won't read it; write with passion; but not so much passion that you scare your audience, even though I know you are trying to follow your passion; make sure you are real and personal with your audience, but not too personal; test different ideas in different posts; don't end a sentence with a preposition; but Star Trek's "to boldly go where no man has gone before" is amazing; you mean to tell me you are gonna be the type of writer that a Trekkie likes; no ands, buts, or because at the beginning of a sentence; make sure you have your outline nailed down before you begin writing; chapter titles are a must and then you write them; your book has to be at least a hundred pages or no one will read it; where is your book marketing plan?; share your book, but don't brag (no one likes that); you (supposedly) can write your book in a weekend; it takes years to write your book; just hire a ghostwriter, it's easier that way; no one will buy your book if you are _____ (a woman, trans, queer, a person of color, below six figures, disabled, never published before, don't have 10K+ followers); know exactly what you want to write before you begin; maybe you aren't ready to write your book.

"Writing Lies" by Shana V. Hartman, Inspired by Jamaica Kincaid's "Girl"

We all have a story about what our books should be like or what our writing should sound like or the best process for getting words on the page. The most lasting and loving piece of advice I can give you is this:

Stop *shoulding* on yourself!

There are already plenty of books out there that seem to fit the system of how one is supposed to _____ (fill-in-the-blank with any number of topics, subjects, goals, how-to guides on writing). These are often drenched in white, patriarchal, cis, heteronormative undertones. In fact, as I write the final lines of this book, we are in the middle of a divisive election year in the United States. I am writing this during a moment in history when many people who fit those above characteristics are fighting tooth and nail to maintain their status quo and keep their privileged voices loud.

Such efforts are not new.

And that's been done. We are over it.

It's *your turn now.*

I deeply hope whenever you are reading this in the near (or far) future, tides have turned. But perhaps they have not. Regardless, we need *your* voice out there in the world in the way that only *you* can say it, presented between two print and/or digital covers in the way that only you could dream up. We are ready for you to blow us away. And you can't do that if you are following a bunch of "what I should do" kinds of tactics and stories about writing and sharing your message. In my final thoughts for this book, I want to make sure you fully understand:

The people I support in writing their books are unique in that writing ignites some kind of spark, some kind of **YES** from deep within that leads them to take the first step and begin offering their thoughts, words, experiences, and expertise to the world.

Writing your book is about activating this spark and igniting a similar fire within you. Write what lights you up! If it lights you up, guess what? Your reader is going to feel that.

In my English professor days, I can't tell you how many times I read a student's essay and thought, "I've read this before." I didn't blame the student for essentially regurgitating the format or words that they had likely written, in some form or fashion, over and over, class after class, because they were taught that "academic" writing *should* look and sound a certain way. The problem is this *should* way of writing was the same for almost every student, often a vanilla carbon copy of formats like the following …

- Write a "hook" sentence to get the reader interested, like "People have been in disagreement about the legalization of marijuana since the dawn of time."
- Share your three main points of your **WHOLE** paper in **ONE** sentence, likely called a thesis statement, at the end of something serving as your introductory paragraph.
- Then take each of those three main points and write one paragraph on each, making sure to have certain types of sentences to introduce, explain, support, and summarize said points. Repeat for the next two paragraphs.
- Finally, end with a summary of all of the above, starting with something like, "In conclusion, one can see …," and try to make it seem like everything that was just said was the smartest thing ever said (even though many have said it before).

Sigh. In those moments, I wanted to run across campus to find the student writer, take them by the shoulders, and say,

"Where are YOU in this writing?" See, as you are now (hopefully) recognizing the writer within and ready to embark or continue your writing journey, you potentially will need to rage against whatever preconceived notions about writing and writing a book you have consciously or unconsciously absorbed over the years. That is why the same question I wanted to ask my students is going to be a very important question to ask yourself in order to keep you, dear writer, from falling into the same trap many of us did as students: where are YOU in this writing?

You are your best resource, expert, and source of inspiration for your words. Period. Why? Because when you are connected to you and your inner truth and wisdom, you are embodied. Embodied writing is the most powerful pathway for honoring the tug, the spark that led you to sit down at the computer or the notebook and begin. Embodied writing is the most powerful way to stay grounded and connected to your words. Embodied writing is the most powerful way to keep going when the "shoulds" I shared throughout this book show up. Embodied writing is how you recognize and bring forth the writer within. Creating embodied writing experiences with my clients is what helped them more easily write and share their core messages from their lives, careers, businesses, and more in empowering books that only they could have written.

Now, it is your turn. I can't wait to read your book.

Write on,

Shana

P.S. Changing your narrative about writing and understanding that writing is *not that* hard is one thing. Since you made it to the end of this book, you are well on your way! However, embodying this idea and (finally) writing the damn thing you know in your soul you are meant to write is a whole other thing. In my experience, this other thing requires powerful support. So I intentionally repurpose the words of evil Ursula from *The Little*

Mermaid and remind you, "My dear, sweet child. **That's** what I do. **It's what I live for**." My team and I would love nothing more than to help you get clear on your next best steps for leaving a legacy with your words! Head to **shanahartman.com/book** to learn more *and* receive some special resources as a reader of my book.

Acknowledgments

How does one write the acknowledgments for a book that feels very much like your life's work? I'm not quite sure. And, as I just wrote a whole book about letting go of the "shoulds" and rules around writing, I am going to do just that and enjoy sending some gratitude out in the world.

To Cindy, my writing ride or die! Thank you times infinity for the 346 reads, the "atta girls," the "how about this?" and "Yes, keep going!" comments all along the way. You helped me keep my eye on the prize, and this book would still be in draft mode if it were not for your support as a part of Team Synergy, but also your support as a friend and writing coach.

To Kemeshia, my editor and reviewer, thank you for affirming what I hoped was a resourceful book to wise educators and writers just like you. Special thanks for making sure my words and sentences were squeaky clean while still sounding like me!

To Charlie and Lydia, thank you for being a reader and reviewer amidst all of the busy in your lives.

To Drs. Jennifer Buckner and Jeanie Reynolds, I am forever grateful that the world of writing, English, and teaching initially connected us, and that our powerful friendship has locked us together forever. Your encouragement and support are palpable on a daily basis.

To Dr. Lil Brannon, I am deeply indebted to how you introduced me to the possibility that there is no one right way to write. My experiences with you in my graduate work and through the National Writing Project forever changed my teaching, my writing, and my life. This book is filled with many echoes of wisdom I learned from you!

To Melisa, thank you for making the cover and interior align with my words!

To my family, I am forever grateful to the four humans who helped wrangle and raise me.

Dad, thanks for always making sure I knew I was your "Big Girl" and from where I came.

Ma, the secret writer, thank you for being my forever cheerleader and keeping up the loving delusion that I am the greatest gift and achievement in your life.

To my stepparents, Mama K and Patty, you are a true testament to how blended, non-traditional families can, indeed, all get along and even love and respect each other. Oh, and thank you for keeping me fed since Dad taught me to cook for myself starting at age seven and Mom limited her cooking to tuna and noodles with raw cookie dough for dessert!

To Jess and Kane, my little sister and brother, while we have been apart more often than we have been together, I am so proud to be your sister and love you dearly. I also love our forever inside jokes about the rest of the hooligans in our family.

To Savanna and Gwen, who will always feel like "my girls" in so many ways. Thank you for indulging me in some of the fun and celebration around this book. You are two of the strongest women I know, and I am forever inspired by both of you.

To my son, Elijah, there are no words that can express how much you mean to me. Your wisdom and humor helped me get to the finish line of this book, whether you knew it or not. Your tweenage snarky comments on my cover design helped me know when I hit the mark! I'll also never forget the way your face lit up when I shared that the preorders had made the book a #1 best seller. A magical mom and son moment! Pure gold.

To all the writers I have had the privilege of working with, whether you were a student or a client, I have learned so much from each of you! Your willingness to put your insides on the outside kept me honest in my journey writing and publishing this book. This book exists because of and for you!

About the Author

Shana V. Hartman, PhD, is a former university English professor turned embodied writing coach. She helps heart-centered professionals and thought leaders share the core messages from their life and career experiences in powerful books by using an embodied writing approach that allows people to truly experience their transformative words. She is a published author many times over and founder and CEO of Synergy Publishing Group. As an ICF certified coach and BodyMind Method© Coach, Shana supports folks in connecting with their inner truth and writing from that place. She truly believes in the power of leaving a legacy with your words. When she's not writing or helping others with their writing, Shana enjoys ballroom dancing, traveling, and spending time with her family.

Learn more about Shana and her work by connecting with her on Instagram @theshana_v. As a thank you for reading this book, you can find additional, no-cost resources and writing guides at shanahartman.com/book.